Dr. Stanley Block has written a revolutionary guide to harnessing our power to heal our body-mind. His techniques are rooted in ancient traditions as well as modern therapies.

DR. MITCHELL GAYNOR, Medical Director and Director of Medical Oncology at Weill Medical College and Cornell University's Center for Complimentary and Integrative Medicine. He is author of *Sounds of Healing* **and** *Healing Essence: A Doctor's Practical Program for Hope and Recovery.*

Bridging the I-System is a brilliant conceptualization of a therapeutic basis for the interaction we caregivers have with families, patients, colleagues, and ourselves. The psychological and spiritual insights Block imparts in straightforward fashion will have a major impact on the management of patients with chemical dependency or other addictions, helping them to be open to change, reducing resistance to care, and avoiding relapses. This "Little Book" is a perfect companion to Alcholics Anonymous' "Big Book." *Bridging the I-System* is must reading for all who are involved in the journey of life.

STANLEY J. EVANS, MD, Clinical Associate Professor of Psychiatry at the University of Vermont Medical School, Medical Director of the Recovery Center, Mercy Hospital and Fellow of the American Society of Addiction Medicine, member Caron Foundation Board of Directors.

Bridging the I-System is an important book brimming with insights. Stanley Block, who practices medicine, psychoanalysis and bridging, presents us with a clear and careful depiction of the I-system, how it facilitates human development up to a point, and then stops its fulfillment. More importantly, Block provides us with wise illustrations and practical guidance for understanding our self (warts and all). But Block does not want readers to settle for mere understanding. Rather he shows how to move ahead into the discovery of the tricks that the I-system plays upon us and then how to overcome these tricks and the fiction of our separateness from Truth or God. Brief but wise, *Bridging the I-System* is a book that deserves wide and frequent readings.

ROBERT TAPP, Ph.D.,Prof. Emeritus of Humanities and Religious Studies, University of Minnesota, Dean of The Humanist Institute, and editor of the book *Ecohumanism.*

Bridging the
I-System

Unifying Spirituality
& Behavior

Bridging the
I-System

Stanley H. Block, M.D.

With Carolyn Bryant Block

WHITE CLOUD PRESS
Ashland, Oregon

First printing: 2002

Cover design by David Rupee, Impact Publications

Printed in Indonesia

Contents

To those of us seeking the truth of our suffering.

PREFACE

WHILE ATTENDING COLLEGE, I began to wrestle with the relationship between God and man—between the unknowable and the knowable. I did not win the match, but I did learn some helpful information surrounding this fundamental topic. For example, I came to understand how the earliest civilizations we know of tried to make the unknowable concrete in structures and idols—in forms they could touch. The ancient Greeks and Romans worshipped mythical deities that were part human and part gods—deities that were humanized and more easily available. The Israelites acknowledged a single creative force, God, who had an unknowable physical form and whose words they documented in the Torah. The Torah laid out an array of laws, ranging from easy interpretations to almost unknowable writings best left to rabbis and mystics. The advent of Jesus—the human form of the unknowable God—brought the unknowable closer to human experience. In another sphere, Buddhism (particularly Zen) acknowledges both the absolute and the relative and proclaims that you and I, like the historical Buddha, can experience both the unknowable and the knowable.

In those days, I even summed up the spectrum of religious activity this way: (1) having one unknowable God and using idols and mythical deities as a bridge to that God; (2) having one unknowable God and using the Written Word, prayer, and deeds of loving kindness as a bridge to that God; (3) having one unknowable God and using His Son as a bridge (using ourselves as living receptacles for Jesus); and (4) using the purified self as a bridge from the unknowable to the knowable. Yet my "bridge" didn't go anywhere.

I wondered how I could use myself as a bridge to absolute certainty, lasting peace of mind, and compassionate action, so I searched for answers in the physical sciences. Early in my training as a theoretical physicist, I learned how systems work. I furthered my knowledge by working as a senior scientist with General Dynamic Corporation, developing guidance systems for missiles and satellites. But I didn't find the answers I was looking for in the physical sciences, so I went back to school at the UCLA Medical School. There, I applied my system theories to biological systems while I worked part-time at the Rand Corporation. During this time, I wrote a paper that was one of the earliest attempts at applying systems theory to human behavior.[1] After graduating from medical school, I pursued a career in psychiatry and psychoanalysis. Despite this success, however, I found that knowledge alone did not give me the peace of mind I sought. The leap in faith from the knowable to the unknowable continued to leave me frustrated.

In another attempt to resolve these big questions, I began practicing self-observation, and I have continued this practice for twenty-five years. Seven years ago, I retired from an active medical practice to devote myself full-time to my search for truth. And the more I searched, the more it became clear that something inside me was resisting my aspirations. I began referring to this resistance as my "I-system." As I explored my own I-system, I discovered a radically new way of understanding my own behavior. I discovered that all of my activities and behaviors were motivated by a spiritual flow from my Source—that is, God—which I could not grasp with my rational mind. Furthermore, my I-system was preventing me from experiencing my spiritual roots. This system also was causing my activities to be out of harmony and balance with our Source. This book, *Bridging the I-System,* is not a psychology or self-help work; instead, it offers a radical process you can use to can melt down your own I-system and expand your awareness. *Bridging* allows your compassionate behavior to flow and peace of mind to abide in your everyday life.

---

1. Stanley H. Block, *A Neural Net for Adaptive Behavior,* Memorandum RM 3808-FR, December 1963, prepared for the United States Air Force by Project Rand, Santa Monica, Calif.

THE PHILOSOPHY OF BRIDGING

W E ARE ALL PART of something, which prior to our
naming it is already here. It is always and forever ours. Let
us call it *Reality*. Because *Reality* is so vast we do not experience it with our mind, which is limited by our self-
centered thoughts (I-System). But we can directly experience *Reality* with our body-mind by simple, everyday
practices, which are called Bridging. Even though *Reality*
is abundantly present in each human being, without the
practice and experience of Bridging it cannot be expressed
(or realized). Bridging unifies the body-mind with our
Source and all existence while purifying our character. We
are then functioning in the state of *Truth* and expressing
Reality in our lives.

TERMINOLOGY

L ET'S BEGIN WITH SOME DEFINITIONS. First, let's talk about what is real. *Reality* has two faces. The material face shows us what we think of as the "real world"—the world we can see with our everyday eyes. By contrast, the non-material (or spiritual) face is what we cannot grasp with our conceptual minds. But we can *experience* this spiritual face, when we allow ourselves to do so. So *reality* in human terms means experiencing both faces and expressing them in our everyday lives. In this book, I will sometimes use words in italics—words like *reality*, *truth*, *action*, *true self*, *ground of existence*, *Source*, *consciousness*, *intelligence*, *seeing*, *compassion*, and *silence*. These terms try to describe a state that unifies both faces—*reality*. For example, we can see a dog with our eyes, but we see the concept of a dog with our minds. *Seeing* can also be extended beyond our eyes or our minds by using our entire body–mind–universe to experience and express the *reality* of the dog. This occurs when we *see* the dog not only as a dog, but as a living entity not apart from us or the universe.

The material face of reality is implied by words like *phenomenal world*, *knowable*, and *relative*. The spiritual face is implied by words like *God*, *absolute*, and *unknowable*. In this understanding:

- Our everyday awareness (or *I consciousness*) both perceives (sees) and conceives (gives birth to) the phenomenal world;
- *Universal consciousness*, when our awareness expands to experience the spiritual world;
- *Consciousness* is simultaneously *I consciousness* and *universal consciousness*; and
- *Bridging* is the activity of our body–mind that allows us to experience and express *reality*.

INTRODUCTION

IN THE PAST FIVE-HUNDRED YEARS, our accumulated knowledge has increased dramatically, but the nature and quality of human behavior has not changed significantly. Violence, cruelty, and other inhumane behaviors are common today. A truly compassionate person, such as Mother Teresa, comes around once in a blue moon. Despite thousands of self-help programs, we continue to miss a true and lasting sense of well-being. Inner turmoil, emptiness, and suffering are everywhere. Faith is tenuous.

The heart of the problem is this: We keep clinging to our I-system. This system is based on the belief in a limited *I* that exists separate from the rest of existence. This belief keeps us from experiencing and expressing the truth of our being and restricts our access to God. The I-system is a hierarchy of self-centered thoughts and emotions whose mission is to uphold the existence of a separate, unchanging, and self-subsistent *I*. Its strength lies in its ability to control our access to awareness. The I-system develops a strategy for completing its mission. Central to this strategy is its ability to generate anxiety. This anxiety happens whenever our existence as a limited *I* is threatened. This signal prompts us to use all of our resources to maintain the I-system's control. Fear is its backbone.

We falsely believe there is no life without our I-system. In fact, we believe we are no more than this limited *I*. This *I* has the ability to feed on itself. Whatever thoughts we have about getting free, opposing the system, or finding our true self are incorporated into the very system we are trying to escape. In fact, the act of trying to outmaneuver or improve the I-system only reinforces its ability to cut us off from our Source. No wonder we can't find satisfaction or peace of mind!

But the I-system does have an Achilles' heel: First, it has a fictional base and, second, it can't function when we are *present in the moment*. So, the path to freedom is knowing the truth about the system and using our inborn awareness to expand our consciousness. This is called bridge building, or *bridging*. Bridging is the passage we create through our body–mind. It can take us from a tension-filled life to one that is filled with harmony and peace of mind.

This book is structured around building bridges. In the first section, I will trace the origins and development of the I-system and look at how it evolves into our personality and restricts our consciousness. Bridging the I-system allows us to expand our awareness into a *universal consciousness*, in which we can experience our true nature. The next section details the workings of the I-system and explores its impact on all the activities of our daily lives—because, you see, all aspects of human behavior are linked to the I-system. The final section develops a step-by-step process that can radically transform your very being.

PART I
THE BLUEPRINT

THE I-SYSTEM

How MANY BOOKS HAVE you read on improving your spiritual, mental, or physical well-being—yet, after a brief honeymoon, you ended up right back where you started? These efforts were bound to fail because they did not address the real problem. We are unfulfilled because the same part of the mind that directs our activities is shutting us off from the only true source of peace and harmony. Following our mind's dictates raises our hopes and expectations, which inevitably ends with frustration and disappointment. This part of the mind is the I-system—a system composed of self-centered thoughts and emotions whose mission is to uphold the existence of a separate, unchanging, and self-subsistent *I*. We are promised a rose garden, then blame the world when we get bloodied by the thorns. Yet we are unaware of the I-system's function and its role in our suffering. Simply being aware of the I-system allows us more choice in following or not following its dictates. As we become familiar with the I-system, we become freer in life's journey.

The I-system is part of our biological system. It is at the top of the body–mind's organizational chart, as shown in Figure 1 (page 7), where it is represented by the small, shaded triangle. The biological system is represented by the larger triangle. Increasing vertical distance from the base indicates higher levels of organization (such as the capacity to process information). At the lowest level are the body–mind's inorganic components (like serum sodium, glucose, etc.), then organic components (like hormones and DNA), cellular systems, organ systems, lower neural systems, higher neural systems, and finally awareness at the top. The I-system is at the very top of the organizational chart and controls our access to awareness and action. Even though it is only a subsystem, it can control the entire biological system.

Let's define some more terminology here: First, a system is a model composed of a set of variables (each of which is a measurable quantity that has a definite value at each instant) used to describe an organism or machine. Each system has a sensory component that measures essential variables the system is trying to regulate. A central segment is programmed to keep the essential variables within certain limits, despite fluctuations in outside conditions.

Think of a simple home heating system. It includes a heater and a thermostat. The thermostat has a thermometer and a switching device that turns the heater on when the temperature drops below a certain number and off when it is above another number. Say we set the temperature at 68 degrees and the thermostat is set to go on at 66 degrees and off at 70 degrees. The mission of the system is to maintain the temperature close to 68 degrees. The key to the system is the feedback loop in the thermostat, which takes information from the sensory component (the thermometer), makes its decision (off at 70 or higher, on at 66 or lower), and sends a message to the motor component (the heater). If everything works, the room temperature stays comfortable, no matter how cold it is outside.

The biological system's mission is to preserve our life and the life of our species. It does this by keeping our biological variables within certain limits. The outer sensory components (like the thermometer) include our eyes, ears, nose, taste buds, and body senses (such as touch, pain, temperature, and position). The inner sensory components measure oxygen, sugar levels, waste production, and so on in the body's fluids, cells, and organs. The outer motor component is our skeletal muscle. The inner motor components are muscles in the stomach, respiratory system, vascular system, and glands. The decision-making components (the feedback loop) include the spinal cord and the brain. For example, when we are in the sun and our internal temperature requirement is breached, we feel hot, so we decide to move into the shade.

The I-system is composed entirely of thoughts that all have one basic mission: to maintain the life of a separate, unchanging, and self-subsistent *I*. Our bodies are connected with the world outside, of course—with air, food, gravity, and water. But the I-system's very existence is founded on our separation not just from the outside world but from the Source of our existence. Our problem comes with this simple fact: We cannot separate ourselves from our Source, any more than a ray of light can separate itself from the sun. Yet the I-system strives mightily to fulfill this impossible mission. It uses its location in the ogranizational chart (at the top) to enforce its belief in separation. The harder the I-System strives the more we feel limited, needy, and constantly unfulfilled. To accomplish its mission, the I-system develops certain core beliefs, which are fueled by the suffering caused by our basic fiction of separation and are a major hidden force directing our lives.[2] An example is, "The world will take care of all my needs."

Each moment the world is the way it is. But our I-System has a picture of how it wants us and the world to be. The details of that picture are our requirements. We want our mate to greet us with a smile. We want our neighbors to be quiet. We don't want our kids to scream. We want to eat what tastes good. We want others to like the way we look. We want to be in shape. We want our hair to be a certain way. We want the latest style. We want to be right. We want to be in control.

When any of these requirements are not met, an internal anxiety alarm is sounded, which prompts us to take action. Anxiety, fear, and tension are hallmarks of the I-sys-

---

2. In her teachings over the past twenty years, Charlotte Joko Beck has developed the ideas of separation, core beliefs, and requirements. Her two published books are *Nothing Special* (New York: Harper Collins, 1993) and *Everyday Zen* (New York: Harper & Row, 1989).

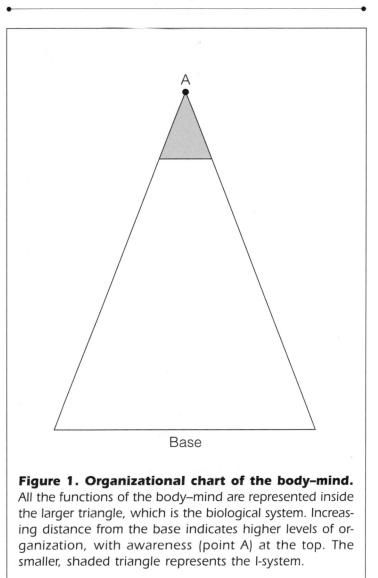

Figure 1. Organizational chart of the body–mind.
All the functions of the body–mind are represented inside
the larger triangle, which is the biological system. Increasing distance from the base indicates higher levels of organization, with awareness (point A) at the top. The
smaller, shaded triangle represents the I-system.

tem. Once developed, the I-system imposes its mission onto our smoothly functioning biological system. But the I-system's attempts to preserve itself can cause great harm to our biological system. Some examples of this are chronic tension, psychosomatic diseases, and addictions of all kinds.

Even though the I-system comes from the Source of all existence, its mission is to maintain separation from that Source and from the rest of existence. It is the most sophisticated system in the universe, but it is based on a fiction. It functions like other systems, but its very existence is based on the idea of a limited *I*—one that exists somewhere inside ourselves. Because it conceives of a separate *I*, it believes that one exists. It's as if the thermostat believed there was a little person inside itself. Our being alive, wondrous, and whole does not depend on there being a limited *I*, of course. On the contrary, this fiction restricts the aliveness, wondrousness, and wholeness of our unlimited self.

The genesis of the I-system parallels the story of Adam and Eve's expulsion from the Garden of Eden. After we bit the apple of knowledge, the I-system emerged and we experienced ourselves as cut off from God. Of course, it was not God who cut us off—that is impossible. It was our belief in a separate, unchanging, self-subsistent *I* that forced us out of the Garden of Eden. But the apple that caused our exile from our Source is the very apple that can lead us back.

REALITY AND CONSCIOUSNESS

W E'VE ALREADY HEARD that *reality* has both a material and a nonmaterial face. The material face is our experience of the outside world, and the nonmaterial face is devoid of characteristics we can perceive or conceive—but they are two sides of one coin—*reality*. One cannot exist without the other. This chapter outlines how we can experience both faces of *reality* by expanding our awareness. But first, let me illustrate the shortcomings of our usual ways of experiencing the world.

Our information from the external world is limited by what we can see, hear, touch, smell, and taste. Because our view is restricted by the way our minds function, we cannot be sure of the real nature of the world, even if we all agree that what we see with our eyes is really "what's out there." Because we don't know that our view is restricted, we believe these limited perceptions are, in fact, *reality*.

But now let's challenge our ideas about the nature of the world. Let's assume that the external world has ten dimensions, instead of the usual three, as some theories of physics now claim.[3] Even if we accept that the world has more than three dimensions, our internal world conception still remains three-dimensional. None of us can conceptualize a four-dimensional cube because of the way our mind functions. So, our conception of the outside world may well be inaccurate and untrue—even if every man, woman, and child on earth agrees with it. We would be like the poor flatworm believing the world is two-dimensional.

Let's look at another example: As humans, we tend to believe there is an absolute time scale by which all events are measured. But this belief is limited by our minds. Einstein's special theory of relativity clearly says there is no absolute duration of time, because any perception of time depends on the observer. Additionally, bridging the I-system demonstrates that time, as we know and love it, is not the complete picture of true time but is limited (like all our perceptions) by our mind's functioning.

Three conclusions from a recent book on modern physics illustrates that the *reality* of our physical universe cannot even exist without our spiritual universe; in other words, the material face of reality cannot exist without the nonmaterial face.[4]

---

3.   Stephen Hawking, Lecture, "The Universe in a Nutshell." March 26, 2001. Seattle, Washington.

4.   Stephen Hawking. *A Brief History of Time* (New York: Bantam Books, 1996).

- First, physicists have demonstrated that particles (such as electrons) have a *wave nature* when they are not under observation, and a *particle nature* when they are. That means, when they are not being watched, particles don't exist as particles. But if a particle isn't being observed, where is it? It can't be in the physical universe, because it does not exist—it only has a probability of existing. In fact, it has a definite probability of being in two different places at the same time. Yet in the physical world, as we all know, one thing cannot exist in two different places.

- Second, it is possible for a particle and its opposite (that is, an electron and a positron) to be created from empty space (a vacuum). But, by definition, a vacuum is empty of particles and anything else. So, where do the particles exist?

- Third, in quantum field theory, all possible histories of the universe exist in imaginary time. Only under certain conditions does a history exist in real time. So tell me, where are all of these imaginary world histories? Where is the imaginary time that physicists have been using in their equations for much of the last century? The only answer is that they are present in the spiritual, nonmaterial universe. Without the spiritual universe, the physical universe could not exist. Nothing appears or disappears in the physical realm unless it goes through the spiritual realm and returns. Because there is constant change in each moment, our physical universe is created anew by God in each moment.

Because everyday awareness can only experience the material universe, we have to expand our consciousness to experience the spiritual universe and *reality*. Generally, we think of consciousness as located at the apex of the brain's functioning. In that model, consciousness screens out the stimuli we don't want and focuses on what we do want. We assume that an *I* is the subject of our awareness—that is, we assume that the content of our awareness is the object itself. Let's refer to this as *I consciousness*. Freud used this model, introducing words like the *subconscious*—referring to material in our mind that's not currently in our awareness but that we can access easily—and the *unconscious*—the material our mind actively pushes away from awareness through repression.[5]

But *reality* is never confined to *I consciousness*. The I-system wants us to believe that our consciousness is limited to what it can grasp: *I consciousness*. Fortunately, we all have the ability to experience not only *I consciousness* but also other, higher versions of consciousness, such as *body–mind* and *universal consciousness*. These three levels of consciousness are illustrated in Figure 2.

To understand *body–mind consciousness*, let's look at the work of Candace Pert.[6] She described how messenger molecules (such as polypeptides, hormones, and neurotransmitters) act in the communication network of the body–

---

5   Sigmund Freud, "The Unconscious." In *Standard Edition of the Complete Works of Sigmund Freud*, vol. XIV, pp. 172–189. (London: Hogarth Press, 1915).

6. Candace Pert, *Molecules of Emotion* (New York: Touchstone Books, 1997).

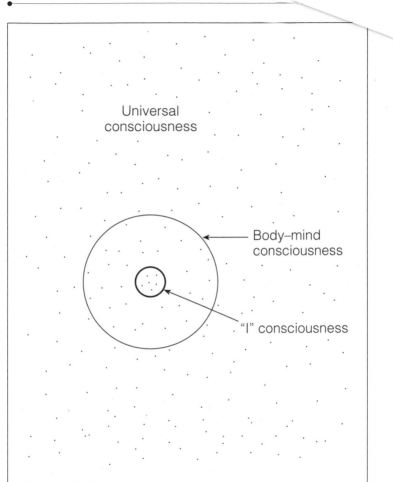

Universal
consciousness

Body–mind
consciousness

"I" consciousness

Figure 2. Consciousness.
You see here the division of consciousness into three
levels. Universal consciousness is represented by the
area that is stippled. Body–mind consciousness is represented by the area within the larger circle. I consciousness is represented by the area within the smaller
circle.

mind. Endorphins (morphine-like substances produced in the body) are the most numerous and potent of these molecules, making up the main communication network of the body–mind. Pert's research demonstrated that each cell of the body has a memory, and that our "brain memory" needs our "body memory" to be complete and accurate. The body is a storehouse of information that enters our awareness and affects our behavior. *Body–mind consciousness* fills the entire body–mind, from head to toe. In fact, as Will Johnson has said, not completely experiencing the body–mind is something like being disembodied.[7] Being cut off from our body sensations limits our ability to experience *body–mind consciousness*.

To understand *universal consciousness*, let's look at some models of the physical world.[8] Using quantum mechanics, physicists today are proposing theories that help to explain the expanding universe. Since the Big Bang (the sudden creation of the universe), fields that affect us today have stretched throughout the universe. These fields and physical laws are manifestations of a *universal consciousness* that exist throughout space and time. The wave-like nature of unobserved particles are also manifestations of *universal consciousness*. Remember, the particle characteristics (that is, the particle nature we can see) are manifested only when *I consciousness* acts—only when the particles are being observed. In each and every moment, *I consciousness*

7. Will Johnson, Change, Transformation, and the Universal Pattern of Myofascial Holding (Unpublished paper).
8. Hawking, *A Brief History of Time.*

acts with *universal consciousness* to make the phenomenal universe appear. Without consciousness, there would be no matter, and without matter, there would be no consciousness. So you see, matter and consciousness are indivisible—one cannot exist without the other.

Now let's look at *I consciousness* from the vantage point of how we see, hear, think, and feel our bodies. If we neglect the minor smell and taste components, the big three of the sensory fields are seeing, hearing, and body sensations. Add to this the mental field of thoughts, and we have four major fields. Now think of a circle divided into fourths (as shown in Figure 3). What our eyes see is in Quadrant 1, what our ears hear is in Quadrant 2, body sensations are in Quadrant 3, and our thoughts in Quadrant 4. The fictional *I* is at the center and is the *subject* of awareness, while the *objects* of awareness occupy the area within our circle of awareness. For example, while I write this I see a yellow pad of paper, my hand, the pen, the table, and my shoe. I hear the refrigerator hum and the door creak. I feel my fingers and thumb on the pen, pressure on my heel, and the pressure of my sitting bones. I think, "Is this clear?" That is my world right now. I experience all of these sensations simultaneously, as the closed circle depicts. You might argue that there is more—such as my dog lying on the floor or thoughts of my wife upstairs—and, of course, there is. You can add anything and everything, but the circle will remain a circle. At any moment in time there can be only one circle of awareness. In the next moment, there is a totally new circle. Because the *I* is constantly changing, the center of the next circle is not at all the center of the first circle. The

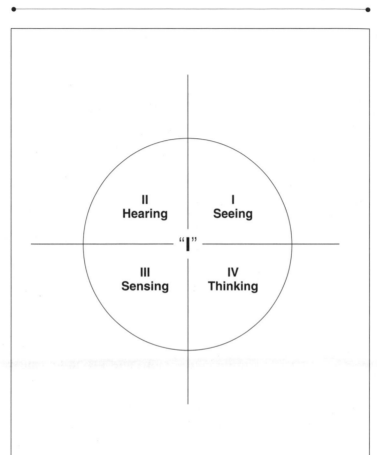

Figure 3. Circle of awareness.
What our eyes see is in Quadrant 1; what our ears hear, in Quadrant 2; what our body senses, in Quadrant 3; and our thoughts, in Quadrant 4. The I at the center is the subject of awareness; the objects of our awareness occupy the area with the circle.

contents of my awareness are all the objects in the circle that make up my world *at this moment*.

Body–mind and *universal consciousness* are always present, of course, but we usually can't experience them because of our I-system. To preserve its belief in separation, the I-system restricts our awareness whenever and wherever it functions. You can experience this if you sit quietly for a few minutes and tune into your circle of awareness (as described in the preceding paragraph). With your awareness not focused on any particular thing, you become aware of a constant background noise, such as traffic sounds or the hum of the refrigerator. If you stay with this for awhile, you will see what happens when your I-system churns out thoughts. The background sounds fade as the I-system restricts your awareness to just thinking.

As the I-system is lessened, our circle of awareness expands and *body–mind consciousness* emerges. Here, the body–mind begins to be experienced *nondualistically*—that is, we experience our body and our mind as not separate from our consciousness. In *body–mind consciousness*, the following changes take place in each of the four quadrants shown in Figure 3. In Quadrant 1, our visual field becomes more relaxed as objects of choice-less awareness float in and out of the field. Usually when we see something, our *I consciousness* makes a choice and grasps at it to the exclusion of all other objects in the field. In *body–mind consciousness*, all of these visual objects are differentiated yet meld together. The same is true for the auditory field; however, our experience is usually less dramatic because we are more familiar with choice-less listening (think of muzak in an elevator or another couple's conversation in a busy restaurant). In Quadrant 3, we can experience our bodies as having light, shimmery sensations that sometimes are experienced first on the face. As embodiment progresses, we feel those light sensations throughout our bodies. It's like we are tuning into the "dance of informational molecules," as described by Candace Pert.[9] Our awareness is accessing the body–mind storehouse of intelligence. The usual dualistic experience of the body—in which our mind, the subject, experiences our body as an object—fades as these new sensations emerge. In Quadrant 4, we experience our thoughts as floating in a field with the sensations from the other senses. Our thoughts don't have the I-system's energy to get organized into our daily drama. Instead, they keep coming and going like raindrops. The I-system's control over our consciousness is lessening.

Universal consciousness develops as we continue to bridge the I-system. Our circle of awareness continues to expand, as shown in Figure 4. In this figure, our awareness starts at *I consciousness*, moves out to *body–mind consciousness*, and then expands to *universal consciousness,* where we experience the universe without separation. *Consciousness* unifies all these levels at the same time. Only *consciousness* knows both faces of *reality*. Bridging is being at home in *universal consciousness* and realizing our existence here and now, in our everyday lives. When we bridge, our daily lives are filled with harmony and balance.

---

9.   Pert, *Molecules of Emotion.*

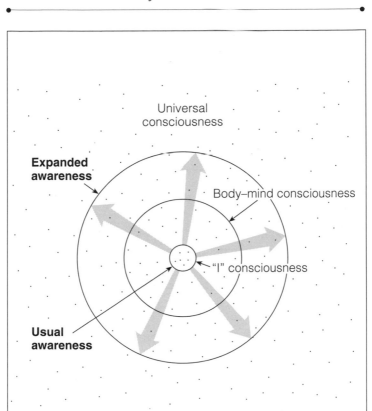

Figure 4. Expanding awareness.
Natural expansion of awareness occurs with bridging.
Our awareness has expanded from our usual level of I
consciousness (shown by the inner circle), through
body–mind consciousness (shown by the larger inner
circle), and includes increasing amounts of universal
consciousness (shown by the stippled area).

DEVELOPMENT OF THE I-SYSTEM

Psychoanalysis, God, and the Soul

O UR BIOLOGICAL SYSTEM is made up of the body–mind work. Each cell, organ, and system has millions of functions that sustain our living activity. One characteristic of human life is that these various functions are unified into a whole by a higher-order functioning. Those unification functions are fewer in number and at a higher level (Figure 1). Our I-system is a stable, cohesive arrangement of functioning that conceives of itself as unchanging, self-subsistent, and separate from everything outside of itself. It is represented by the shaded area in Figure 1. It's as if a part of the biological system has masterminded a bloodless takeover and seized power.

But the I-system is different from the common idea of the *ego*. In everyday use, ego connotes excess pride, pompousness, or an inflated sense of self. Our I-system may contain these thoughts, but it also includes the exact opposite thoughts, as well as all other personality characteristics. Those with minimal pride and pompousness (those who have "small egos") still have big I-systems that cling to the idea of separation.

In psychoanalytic theory, the ego is characterized by many functions, including perception, thinking, feeling, controlling impulses, managing relationships, and regulating self-esteem. The ego's features are determined by how it has used its biological predisposition in adapting to its environment. The goal of psychoanalysis is to improve our ego functions and to expand ego activities. By contrast, the I-system is organized solely around maintaining its separation. Bridging is an I-system meltdown, leading to true freedom of mind and body function.

In Kohut's theory of psychoanalysis, the self is a system that is nurtured by important relationships with others (such as mother, father, teachers, siblings, and friends).[10] Appropriate nurturing relationships at the right ages, combined with our genetic potential, create a relatively stable, self-nurturing, and adaptive self. When the self-system functions well, the body's mental functions are maintained well. Conversely, a poorly developed or malfunctioning self-system is associated with impaired mental functioning. One goal of psychotherapy is to have the patient experience a stable and more nurturing self. This improves his self-esteem and mental functioning. Kohut's stable and self-

---

10. Heinz Kohut, *Analysis of the Self* (New York: International University Press, 1971).

nurturing self is the highest level of development allowed by the I-system. With bridging, our awareness expands through *body–mind consciousness,* and the functioning of the self-system improves as our entire body–mind is integrated in a nondualistic fashion into the self-system. Our bodies are no longer treated as objects; our thoughts and actions are less self-centered. In *universal consciousness,* the limited self expands into the true self. The true self is not self-nurturing but is nurtured by and nurtures all existence. Our actions are rooted in the moment, instead of in the I-system's need to maintain separation. So the self becomes *true self* as we experience and express ourselves in the spiritual and material realms of *reality.*

All the creative forces that gave rise to our development as a species shaped the development of the I-system. Although the I-system keeps us from experiencing our true nature, it must have had adaptive and survival benefits for the human species, because it is so central and so deeply entrenched. Free choice, essential to the I-system, allows us to learn and survive as a species. Rather than having a simple, predetermined reflex between sensory input and motor output, humans have a higher order of neural activity. We remember a particular motor output that benefits the organism and we associate it with a particular sensory input. Thus, we gain the benefit of learning by trial and error.

At some point in human development, our brains learned to envision action and eventually to plan. Human communication evolved through signing and then through speech. We then developed an ability to conceive of a separate body–mind. To conceptualize an *I* separate from you and the phenomenal world—that is the necessary condition for the I-system. When we believe these conceptions, we create the right conditions for the I-system to flourish. Although thoughts are originated in the biological system, the I-system selectively confiscates them for its own purpose. Once we believe the I-system, its thoughts control our behavior by creating and reducing anxiety.

Our interaction with our Source is present each and every step along the way, despite the I-system's portrayal. If we did not believe the I-system's fiction of separation, we wouldn't need to reunite—because we wouldn't be separated in the first place. So, we wouldn't need spirituality or religion in any form. Instead, we would experience and express our union with God in each and every moment. What else can religion promise?

The soul is the bridge between us and our Creator. In the Garden of Eden, there was no I-system, no separation, and no soul. You see, either we have a soul, or we are in perfect union with God. An interesting story asks whether humans or the angels are more holy. After months of arduous discussion, the elders in the story decided that humans were more holy. They reasoned that because humans have souls, they have a holy mission to perform—to reunite with God. The angels are already in God's Court, lightened by the absence of a soul.

The rain joyfully acknowledges its Source with each drop, the snow with each flake, and the ocean with every grain of salt and molecule of water. Only we, who conceive of ourselves as separate, need religion, reunion with

God. Because the raindrops, snowflakes, waves, rocks, apples, birds, and animals all absolutely express their Source in each moment of life, what need do they have for a soul? The soul exists only because we deny our union with the Divine—because we cannot experience and express it in each moment. An apple has no soul. It expresses the grandeur of its Source each moment. Do we? Of course we don't. So we need an interface, a soul.

Bridging assumes that each of us has an I-system. Is it possible for a person to grow up without an I-system? For that to happen, a baby's consciousness would have to be so expanded that any attempts to believe in the idea of separation would fail. This expanded consciousness would not allow any separation between the baby and God. So *I* worship would fail. There would be ideas of separation, permanence, and self-subsistence, but no false beliefs, no fear, no I-system. The highest components of the baby's biological system would function in harmony with itself, its source, and all existence. However, with a few historical exceptions, most people's I-systems form quite nicely during infancy.

At birth, the newborn mind is rudimentary. The baby cannot organize her experiences of her body and the world into verbal concepts. Pleasure and pain attract her awareness and create preverbal mental and physical activity. However, pain is accompanied by unpleasant mental activity and body tension. When a subject, *I*, is attributed to the pain experience, the baby has a beginning I-system. Primitive thought and sensory activity, as well as related motor activity avoiding this pain, become associated with the rudimentary I-system. These unpleasant experiences provide the foundation of the I-system because they attract the baby's consciousness and begin controlling her body.[11]

As the baby matures and develops, the I-system begins to take hold. At six months, the newly formed *I* has the baby believing in her separate, unchanging, self-subsistent *I*. If we put our six-month-old, nonverbal I-system into words, the core belief could be this: *I am entitled solely to pleasure.* Experiences of pleasure cause relaxation and calmness, whereas pain causes tension, furious kicking, arm flailing, head banging, and crying. As the baby grows, her requirements develop, so her I-system expands. For example, seeing her mother leave the room causes the baby anxiety. She needs her mother to be close by for calmness. The baby has additional requirements: no strange people or surroundings, no darkness, no startling noises, no wet or cold skin, no thoughts that "Mother will leave." If any one of these requirements is violated, the baby experiences anxious thoughts and sensations, such as rapid pulse, shallow breathing, and excessive muscular activity. Thus we have a full-blown, primitive I-system.

So, by six months we all have a personal I-system, with a basic fiction of separation and a core belief that "I am entitled solely to pleasure." We also have a unique set of requirements for the outside world to fulfill. The resulting frustration leads the I-system to develop more complicated strategies to fulfill its requirements and core belief. For ex-

---

11. For readers interested in the development of the *I* during infancy, see addendum at end of this chapter.

ample, when mother turns her back, the baby may cry. This activity is aimed at ensuring that mother remains close by. The baby's personality is evolving.

The basic fiction, "I am separate, unchanging, and self-subsistent" remains unchanged in all adults. But our core beliefs, requirements, and personalities become unique and individual. My own core belief might be "There is a good mother (or person) who will take care of me," or "All my pain is caused because I am not good enough." Another core belief, "The world will fulfill all my needs," might lead to requirements like these:

- My spouse will always be attentive to me and consider my needs before hers.
- My job will be easy and well paid.
- My stock market investment will only go up.
- My kids will not cause me any trouble.
- People will always be nice to me.
- I will have sex three times a week.
- I will not have to wait in lines.
- I will not get sick.
- The roof will never leak.
- Murphy's Law does not apply to me.

Our personalities are woven around our attempts to satisfy these insatiable requirements. Some examples of personality traits associated with the requirement for an attentive spouse are: be bossy, be self-confident, be demanding or be extra kind in hopes that she will reciprocate. Some other personality traits are listed below:

- Be an obsessive and compulsive worker and re-main bitter, because life isn't easy.
- Keep changing jobs, looking for greener pastures.
- Keep taking needless risks.
- Be frightened of risky behavior and be very con-servative.
- Be a great parent.
- Create so many rules that the children must rebel.
- Keep so busy with your own activities that the kids' behavior will not bother you.

Obviously, personality development is complicated and involves every aspect of the body–mind and the environment. What I want to stress here is that our core beliefs, requirements, and strategies are parts of normal personality development in our culture. They may be adaptive, and they are not meant to convey mental illness or disorder.

FOR THOSE INTERESTED IN EARLY *I* DEVELOPMENT

D URING THE FIRST SIX MONTHS of life, the inside and outside of the body–mind aren't differentiated, and the baby's inner world is filled with preverbal fantasies about what he experiences. If we could put these fantasies into words, they would sound something like this: "Everything that comes into my awareness *is me*"—that is, *I am* everything my body–mind takes in through my eyes, ears, mouth, nose, feelings, and thoughts. Because inside and outside are not differentiated, mother—her eyes, her breast or the bottle, her smile—is part of me, part of the *I*. As mother comes and goes, then, the baby experiences taking parts of mother into his *I* and losing other parts. Taking food into his mouth causes the food to disappear and brings on other sensations, such as pleasure. In this way, children learn to incorporate parts of the outside world into the *I*. For this to happen, however, we need to differentiate the inner and outer worlds. Vomiting or spitting out food may be a physical model for getting rid of or projecting parts of the *I*. As the baby develops, his inner and outer worlds become more clearly differentiated. Now he can have an inner representation of self and objects (others). At first, he considered the mother who causes pleasure separate from the mother who causes displeasure. Now, he has an inner representation of the "good mother" and the "bad mother."[12] Normal growth and development lead to the next stage, called *object constancy*, in which the inner representation is a fusion of the good and bad mothers. The baby learns that the same mother who frustrates gives pleasure. Before this stage, the baby's relationships are with partial objects (good or bad mother or parts of mother's body). Once this stage has been reached (at six months or so), basic trust has been developed. This means that mother's actions can lead to displeasure, but the baby still maintains a positive mental image of the mother.

The preverbal conception of a subject and object is the birth of our *I*. If there were no conceptions, only physical and mental sensations, there would be no *I*. Preverbal perceptions of the world (e.g., mother's hands, breasts, and eyes) are mixed with body sensations and early mental ideas. These images, sensations, and prethoughts are organized around a subject *I* whose existence is experienced as separate from the outside world. In addition, the baby experiences his *I* as unchanging and self-generated. So, we have the basis for the I-system.

---

12. Melanie Klein, *Psychoanalysis of Children* (London: Karnac Books, 1998).

SYNTHETIC FUNCTIONING AND PERSONALITY:

SEPARATE BUT ONE

THERE IS NO EXISTENCE without *synthesis*—the making of a whole from separate and diverse parts. Synthetic functioning brings all the diverse body-mind functions into one, harmonic whole: All sights, sounds, thoughts, and body sensations are synthesized into one awareness. In each moment there is only one awareness. If you are present in this very moment, the entire universe is present, too. One cannot exist without the other, because in each moment, the entire universe is created all together—because of universal synthetic functioning. An apple has a complete and whole "appleness." Each apple seed has its own complete and whole "seedness." The same is true for each bite of the apple. Synthesis creates a complete universe from indivisible, whole parts. Everything in creation has synthesis.

Every cell, every organ system, and our complete body–mind all have synthetic functioning. Even our dualistic thinking, which tries to separate good and bad, me and you, up and down, is synthetic, linking opposite thoughts despite our best efforts. In synthesis, God is whole and complete, and humans are whole and complete. At the same time, God–and–humans become an indivisible unit by synthesis. The I-system embraces synthesis when it comes to organizing itself into a unit, but it opposes synthesis by denying its own unity with its *Source*. Our I-system's insistence on separation is the root of our personality—no separation, no personality. Most of us think, "But how can I 'be' without my personality?"

Because of this basic fiction of separation, we experience and suffer a loss of union with God. We artificially cut ourselves off from our *Source*. In effect, we dissect our true selves by rejecting our spiritual reality, and so we constantly cause each and every cell of our body–mind to suffer. This is the price we pay for an I-system. But what makes this suffering situation a divine comedy is that, in reality, *we are never separated*.

All of our core beliefs are fueled by the pain of separation and the loss of wholeness and completeness. Remember the adult core beliefs from the last chapter:

1. The world will fulfill all my needs.
2. There is a good mate or friend who will take care of me.
3. All my pain is caused because I am not good enough.

In the first, the emptiness caused by separation fires the belief that somehow the world will fill up our bottomless void. But the void continues, so the pressure on this core belief is unrelenting. In the second, the emptiness fuels a desire for someone to give us constant nurturing. But our void is never filled, so the search continues. In the third, we blame the pain of separation on ourselves.

Figure 5 is an illustration of the I-system. The basic fiction is the belief in the thought "I am separate," which is the central ring and constantly reinforces the *I* as the center of the world. The core belief (for example, the world will fulfill all my needs) is the *I*'s mission statement and directs our behavior. The requirements in the next ring show how that mission statement gets carried out in the world. For example, for the baby, having mother close by is a requirement. When these requirements aren't fulfilled, we feel anxiety. This anxiety signals the I-system to find ways of fulfilling our requirements or forming new ones. Our personality is the strategy we develop for fulfilling our requirements. That strategy involves our entire body–mind. Let's call our mental components *personality traits* and our bodily components *somatic traits*. Our synthetic functioning integrates all of these components, no matter how different they are, into our personality.

Figure 6 (p. 34) shows the structure of a seven-year-old boy's I-system with the core belief, "The world will fulfill all my needs." The child has four requirements:

1. My mother will always be attentive.
2. My father will give me things I want.
3. My friends will like me.

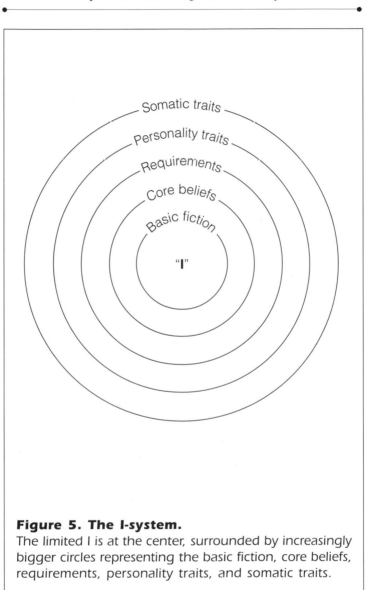

Figure 5. The I-system.
The limited I is at the center, surrounded by increasingly bigger circles representing the basic fiction, core beliefs, requirements, personality traits, and somatic traits.

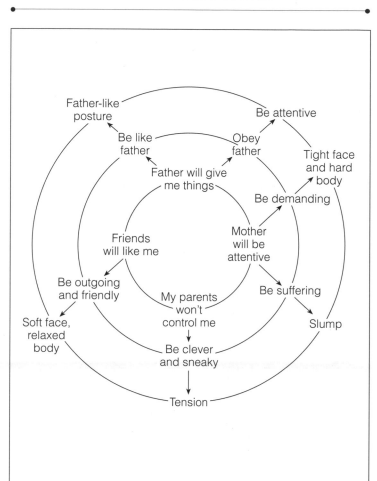

Figure 6. A seven-year-old's I-System.
The outer circle carries the somatic traits; the middle circle, the personality traits; and the inner cirlce, the system's requirements. The arrows show the relationship between elements in the circle's circles. The core belief and basic fiction are not shown.

4. My parents won't control me.

These requirements fulfill his I-system's mission statement—that the world will fulfill all his needs. Two personality traits are associated with the first requirement:

1a. Be demanding of attention with mother and with mother figures.
1b. If I don't get the attention I need, try to squeeze it out of her by suffering a little or a lot.

Two more personality traits are associated with number 2:

2a. Do what father says.
2b. Be like father.

Another personality trait is associated with number 3:

3a. Be outgoing and friendly only with kids I like.

Finally, one personality trait is associated with number 4:

4a. Be clever and sneaky.

Although these traits seem contradictory, the I-system's synthetic functioning pulls all the pieces together, with each personality trait there is at least one associated somatic trait. So, the boy's somatic traits are these:

1a. A tight face and hard body
1b. A "slumped over" posture

2a. Attentiveness
2b. A father-like posture
3a. A soft friendly face, relaxed body
4a. Tension

Many of our personality traits have unconscious components, and all of our somatic traits have them. Thus, the I-system functions at both a conscious and an unconscious level, although the greatest part is unconscious.

Personality formation is driven by the fires of separation. Of course, our temperament, environment, and many other things contribute to our personality, but only one thing causes its existence: our belief in the basic fiction, "I am separate, unchanging, and self-subsistent." Your I-system's synthetic functioning brings together all your personality and somatic traits into your whole personality. But each personality trait has an opposite lurking somewhere. Typically, we repress or deny these opposite traits. We expose our somatic and personality traits to the outside world; the way we interact with it—by walking, thinking, and acting—is determined by these traits.

Your I-system and your personality are two sides of the same coin: Personality is the outer aspect, and the I-system is the inner. Synthesis unifies both aspects. Our personality is nothing more than bits and pieces of ancient memories — old identifications with the people we have loved or feared; habitual patterns of thoughts and muscular activity, and past frozen reactions to feelings of weakness, shame, helplessness, anxiety, guilt, and pleasure. All of these memories are unified by our synthetic functioning. Our personality is based on our self-centered activities. If we looked at each part clearly, we probably would reject most of them. But the I-system has us hanging onto every bit and piece for dear life.

So, our personality is based on old mental and physical memories *that are not present in the reality of the moment.* Think of your I-system and personality as a mask that you put over your real face. What's left when you remove the mask? Your body–mind freely functioning in everyday life—your magnificent true self is left.

BRIDGING AS LIFE'S PRACTICE

WRITER YITZCHAK GINSBURGH has beautifully described the underlying meaning of bridging this way:

> The soul's spiritual search for the Truth—to reach aware-
> ness of the Divine Presence permeating all reality, to sense
> God's Infinite Transcendence, until ultimately to perceive
> (in faith) the absolute Unity of Transcendence and Imma-
> nence.[13]

Bridging is not something you do for "self-improve-
ment." It is a holy pursuit of *truth*. Before humans bit the
apple of knowledge, they had no I-system. Adam and Eve

---

13 Yitzchak Ginsburgh, *I am Asleep Yet My Heart is Awake*
(Jerusalem: Gal Einai, 1984), p. 48.

were *present* in each moment and realized their *presencing* with God. They knew their place in both *transcendence* and *immanence*. They bridged in each and every moment. With that first bite of self-centered knowledge—the advent of the I-system—a major obstacle to bridging emerged.

Bridging means gratefully receiving and joyfully expressing our *being* in each moment. Because of the I-system's fiction of separation and its restriction of our awareness, we do not often experience this natural event. You see, the I-system's existence is based completely on false beliefs, and so it resists efforts at bridging. Of course, the I-system can no more close us off from our Source than a ray of light can cut itself off from the sun. But the I-system is the grandest system in the universe, and it uses all of its resources (including your biological system) to accomplish its mission of separation. It constricts our awareness, so that our body–mind does not experience the creative energy coming from our Source—the energy of God creating all existence anew in each and every moment. Our I-system has us believing that "our" energy is separate, unchanging, and self-subsistent. In effect, it has us wearing blinders that keep us from seeing the truth—that our energy and the energy of God and the universe are the same.

The root of our suffering is our belief in our separateness. The I-system tenses our body–mind to mask our pain. This tension (and the resulting lack of normal body sensation) is *disembodiment*. Because of the I-System's mask we wear, we are not even aware of our deep and ever-present suffering. The I-system uses this suffering to propel its own activities, convincing us that fulfilling its requirements is the ticket to success. And so our suffering continues. Each cell of our body–mind *knows* that we are not really separate from our Source and all existence, so we aspire to see the truth, to expand our consciousness, which the I-system opposes. Our aspirations are simply manifestations of our souls thirsting for reunion with our Source. This is the basis of faith, but this faith cannot be conceived by the I-system, *which does not believe that our aspirations exist.*

Because the I-system oppose bridging, we need ways to get around the system—we must play on the system's weakness. And we're in luck: The I-system has three weaknesses. First, the entire system is based on false thoughts that we choose to believe. Second, because the system's power is based solely on thinking, it cannot function in periods of silence, when we are present in the moment. Third, we can weaken the system's ability to control us by practicing *choice-less* or *nonfocused awareness.*

For bridging we must be mindful of the following:

1. *I consciousness* splits us apart from *consciousness* and creates the I-system, which falsely points us away from our Source. This creates disharmony and un-balance. We are separate and not separate at the same time. Bridging allows us to find and unify our place in both the *transcendent* (not separate) and the *immanent* (separate) realms.

2. We cannot accomplish bridging with our rational minds. Yet thinking does not disappear with bridging. Instead, it becomes unfettered and begins to function freely.

3. *Choice-less awareness* expands our consciousness and allows us to *see* the *truth* and fulfill our souls' aspirations. Once we see our place in *transcendence*, bridging actualizes the *truth* in everyday life, thus securing our place in *immanence*.

4. Bridging is practice, and practice is using our body–minds. Our life is nothing other than our body–minds functioning. Bridging is practicing harmony and balance with both faces of *reality*. Practice rests on a physical base. First, we harmonize and balance our bodies. Next, we harmonize our minds. Finally, we harmonize our *body–mind– universe* with *reality* and express that *truth* in *action* in our everyday lives.

5. In everyday life, bridging is simply experiencing our thoughts, perceptions, and body sensations when the requirements of the I-system are frustrated or satisfied. Bridging is quietly watching our I-system churn out spiteful thoughts and tension when we visit an unpleasant relative.

Before discussing these different levels of practice, let's consider a line from one of Bach's chorales: "In Thine arms I lay me down to rest."

On the physical level:

*   "In Thine arms" represents your immediate surroundings: for example, your chair, gravity, the space in the room, the furniture, and other people nearby.

*   "I lay me down" refers to harmonizing and balancing your body as you sit, stand, walk, or lie on the couch.

- "To rest" implies relaxing, stopping the body activities not needed to keep your current posture. Relaxation is effective only with alignment and resilience.[14] *Alignment* means using the body's senses to adjust your posture within gravity. You position your backbone so that minimal effort is needed to keep your posture. *Resilience* (or elasticity) is the body's flexibility, which allows your breathing to move even the sutures in your skull. Everyday activities take place more smoothly when you practice alignment resilience.

Now let's go a bit deeper:

- "In Thine arms" represents the perceptions, thoughts, and sensations that are constantly coming and going in your body–mind.

- "I lay me down" also means finding an inner place of tranquility where you can make your observations. Without this peaceful spot, it's nearly impossible to calmly watch your hectic mental and physical activities.

- "To rest" means resting in the present moment with *choice-less awareness* of your perceptions, thoughts, body sensations, and actions. It means resting your

---

14. For readers interested in a full elaboration of these concepts, Will Johnson's *Aligned, Relaxed and Resilient: The Physical Foundations of Mindfulness* (Boston: Shambhala Publications, 2000) is helpful.

Bridging as Life's Practice

I-system so that your body–mind activities can run smoothly.

On the deepest level, Bach's chorale sings like the Mormon Tabernacle choir.

- "In Thine arms" represents your life. This includes not only everything within your present awareness, but other conditions of your internal and external worlds. It includes your genetics, birth, upbringing, family, friends, job, education, and so on.

- "I lay me down to rest" seems passive at first glance, but in the deepest sense it means activity within calmness and stillness. It means you have found your ground of existence, your true nature, and have resumed your everyday activities securely held in God's arms. This is what I call bridging. This is the practice of true living.

43

PART II
CONSTRUCTION

WORKING WITH YOUR I-SYSTEM

THE PREVIOUS SECTION established a framework for investigating the I-system. This section paints broad-brush pictures of the I-system in action. Initially, we are so identified with our I-system we don't even know it exists. Expanding our awareness of it automatically brings us closer to our Source and allows us to live our everyday lives in more harmony and balance. Bear in mind a few points while you read this section:

1. The I-system is your "friend," your partner in everyday life. When you encounter its activity in your life, try to be kind, gentle, and patient—maybe even give it a name. Remember, there is no gateway to your Source without this friend.

2. Being present in the moment means simply being aware of the four fields (seeing, hearing, thinking,

body sensations)—no more, no less. This awareness is the ground on which your body–mind relaxes and your mind quiets even in the middle of activities.

3. Awareness is your natural state. You are not separate from consciousness or matter. Choice-less awareness is being present in each moment with non-focused attention. Choice-less awareness of the I-system always expands your consciousness.

4. The I-system's power comes from its ability to restrict your awareness, which makes it hard to expand your consciousness.

5. Remember that thoughts originate in the biological system. Our I-system confiscates thoughts to fulfill its mission. Expanding our awareness limits this I-system activity.

6. Times when you have incessant thinking or body tension are prime times to view your I-system. Quietly observe these thoughts and body sensations as your friend works.

7 When you are upset, return again and again to mindfulness of your body sensations and everyday sounds.

8. To gain the clearest view of your I-system, try experiencing your body–mind when its requirements are unfulfilled.

9. Your friend wants you to believe that satisfaction of its requirements is home, but your true home

is functioning freely in the present moment.

10. Bridging allows our awareness to become a *knowing* that flows in the doings of our everyday life. Our doing is for no other purpose than to express our true nature as a manifestation of God's grandeur on earth.

LIFE AND DEATH

WHEN THE BUDDHA was a boy, his father (a king) had the palace workforce remove all signs of old age, sickness, and death to shield the child. It was only as a young man, when he first saw human suffering, that the Buddha began his quest for understanding and truth. Like Buddha's well-meaning father, we are constantly shielding ourselves from suffering. Most of us say, "Why should I suffer?" But by building an artificial barrier in our minds, we actually give energy to the misery we are trying not to see. Trying to "not think" about a thing only energizes that thing. Shielding ourselves from suffering by denying and repressing our natural thoughts and sensations prevents us from living full lives. Openly dealing with death allows us to realize life. Denying death takes inordinate amounts of body–mind energy. To freely and fully partake in the life we are given, we must be aware of our life's circumstances: the greater our awareness, the greater our freedom.

Universal consciousness contains every thing in harmony and unity. The phenomenal world appears in our *I consciousness* in each moment. Then the I-system experiences the world as an object and splits it into desirable (good) and undesirable (bad) parts. So, the rain is good if the garden is dry but bad if we are planning a picnic. But the I-system goes further: it splits our body–mind as well—so we have a "good" side and a "bad" side. Shame and guilt are the results of this self-condemnation.

The I-system believes it can do away with the bad elements; but it is impossible to conceive of anything without its opposite (good/bad, up/down, heaven/hell, life/death, saint/sinner, hard/easy, beautiful/ugly). Whenever we conceive one element in the *I consciousness*, the other is energized in the unconscious. This is why the I-system can never give us peace of mind, because the opposite thought—which we label as bad—is always lurking in our unconscious. The I-system then uses its resources and energy to repress these opposites. So, although the I-system has a conception of life and death, we repress or deny its full emotional impact.

Because *universal consciousness* contains absolutely everything and *I consciousness* takes in only half of the created pair, the opposite half is left active in our unconscious, constantly creating tension. Because *life* includes both life and death, embracing life and rejecting death creates tension. Only by reuniting these opposites can we release the tension.

Let me elaborate here on a universal principle that most of us readily accept: Everything changes. Nothing maintains its identity for even a moment. What our I-system calls an apple or a self changes in each moment. Rational thinking limits this dynamic *alive* quality. When we rationally think of an apple, we separate it from its surroundings and source. Our cognitive mind assumes there is something that maintains its identity for a period of time. It also assumes that a thing has boundaries and can maintain its identity separate from everything else—that it is self-subsistent. But is there really an unchanging apple or a self separate from the universe? The I-system assumes that there is a self within us that is separate, self-subsistent, and unchanging. But we know this is not true. The separate self does not exist, does not live, and does not die. Although some of us might accept this as an idea, we can only feel the certitude and the peace of this conviction when we taste the unification of *life* and *death* with our entire body–mind.

So *life* is an organic whole; life and death are inseparable. Our I-system clings to life and denies its unity with death. Rather than acknowledging that everything changes, our I-system holds onto its false concept—*I* am separate and unchanging—and tries to shield itself from death. But this action only ensures that death is constantly energized and always lurking behind us. And so we are terrified of death.

Most of us will admit that we are all going to die, but

the I-system greatly resists this conclusion. Yet the system cannot imagine true life (*life*) or true death (*death*); all it can see is its own demise, which has nothing to do with *life* or *death*. The system's life is a drama of avoiding pain and seeking pleasure based on a web of false beliefs. It spins this web using requirements that seek out half the world and reject the rest. The body–mind is a victim of the system's denial, because the denial is always accompanied by tension. The I-system is responsible for just about all the problems we have in dealing with death. It also interferes with our fully living because it prevents us from experiencing all aspects of *life*.

Imagine a loved one's pending death. Usually, your I-system refuses to face such a loss. As long as the system resists the truth, you consume energy in useless resisting activities. When you think about the dying person, your body experiences enormous tension. You may choke up, feel tightness in your throat and chest, breathe shallowly and rapidly. You may have cramps in the lower abdomen or burning in the stomach. Your bridging task is to simply allow and experience these feelings. Be as aware as possible of all the experiences that life is bringing in each moment. The larger your container of awareness, the better your bridging. Simultaneously including your lonely thoughts and painful sensations along with everyday sounds and sights is most helpful.

As your loved one's illness ends with death, your emotional and cognitive storm intensifies. But even now, your practice must continue. The practice is simple and effective, but because of the I-system's resistance, it can be very hard. Facing a loved one's death brings up the subject of our own demise. If you can overcome your resistance, painful thoughts about your own life's end rush to the forefront. But as you allow in more feelings of loss and sadness, your awareness expands. As you become more aware of the central role that fear of death plays in your life, that fear's hold on you diminishes. With time, you will come to a bigger version of who you are—a true self that is both changing and unchanging in the midst of continuous change, one that does not disappear with disappearances or appear with appearances.

Then, you can boldly meet life and death as they blossom in each moment. Fortunately, you don't have to wait for life's end to start bridging your I-system. As you become more aware of the system, you can see that its life depends on constantly reinforcing its concepts of life and death: It energizes death by fear, denial, addictions, and dangerous behavior; and energizes it's limited idea of life by preoccupation with health and the self's welfare. As our belief in the system's limited concepts of life and death is lessened, we are released to a greater awareness. At the moment of our birth, nothing is added to our true self. At the moment of our death, nothing is taken away. Life is a total manifestation of *life*. Death is a total manifestation of *death*. Life does not change into death. Because all the befores and afters are present in the moment of death, it is not the extinction of something preceding it.[15]

---

15. Joan Stambaugh, *Impermanence is Buddha Nature* (Honolulu: University of Hawaii Press, 1990), Chap. 4.

LIFE IS MOMENTARY

LIFE IS COMPOSED solely of the functions of each moment: cells connecting, muscles contracting, blood carrying oxygen, wind moving, dogs barking, flowers blossoming. Life is the momentary manifestation of universal total functioning. But of course, our rational mind does not grasp this functioning, which creates the entire universe anew in each moment. The I-system fools us into believing that our life contains a continuous series of moments, starting with our birth and ending so many years later with our death. Not experiencing life in the moment removes us not just from God but from *life*—because *life* is in the moment.

The I-system fools us into believing we can act in the past and the future. All activities take place only in the present. This present moment is completely cut off from moments before and after. We are alive here and now in this very moment because of our body–mind and our

Source. Yesterday's heartbeat won't keep us alive today. Once something has happened, it can never be undone. Once we burp, we can't take it back. All we can say is, "Excuse me." We can't avert an accident after the fact. Conversely, we can never perform an action before its time. Your heart can't pump tomorrow's blood until tomorrow. You can practice foul shoots with a basketball hundreds of times, but when the crucial moment comes in the game, only that shot counts. Your entire life is *whole* and *real* only in the present moment. Life is momentary rather than continuous.

At this moment, your eyes are gazing at the words on this page, your body–mind is alive with other sensations and perceptions. Your synthetic functioning gathers everything together into one awareness. Whatever exists in this *page–moment* is a complete realization of *reality*. Your existence, the page, the moment, and everything else are not separate. Time and existence are not two. We are not separate from time or the moment. Of course, the I-system conceives of time and the book page as separate from us, but experiencing only the material face of *reality* always creates tension, anxiety, and fear. For example, we are always fearful of time passing by.

The spiritual face of the present moment is inconceivable to the rational mind. The present moment is a gathering together and realization of everything that is, ever was, or ever will be. Nothing is missing. For example, you see this page has white paper and black ink formed into letters. But the true *page* doesn't just have white paper and blank ink; it includes you, the present moment, and the sun, clouds, rain, earth, and tree that went into the paper. It includes the entire history of civilization and the universe. The print contains ink *and* the history of ink; the letters include the history of language, the writer's life, his teachers, his parents, and on and on and on. In fact, the true *page* includes everything our rational mind would consider "not page," because everything in existence is present in the moment in the spiritual face of *reality*.

Although whatever is realized in the moment doesn't keep its identity for even that moment, it does not "change" into whatever is realized in the next moment. What is present in the moment is eternal. The true *tree* does not disappear or change when we witness its wood being made into paper. *Tree* is a total and complete realization of *reality*. *Paper* is a total and complete realization of *reality*. When paper appears as the material face of reality, the remainder of *existence*, inlcuding the tree, is present as the spiritual face of *reality*, even if our eyes don't see it. Likewise, true *time* contains all of time—past, present, and future. Our perception of the present moment is the material face of *reality*; all other moments are the nonmaterial face of *reality*. The moment itself is eternal. Most of us think of our lives as containing moments, *but life is in the moment*. Time never passes us by.[16]

Residuals of the I-system that exist beyond our awareness prevent us from fully experiencing the moment. This causes our actions to be out of harmony and balance with

---

16. For those interested in a fuller understanding of temporality, see Joan Stambaugh's *Impermanence Is Buddha Nature*.

reality. But we have a renewed opportunity to return to *being in the moment* if we expand our consciousness to include the actions prompted by our I-system. Thus, the I-system continually gives us new bridging opportunities. By repeating the process of *being present in the moment* again and again, we gradually expand our awareness and shrink the I-system. By doing so, we experience and express ourselves in increasing harmony with *reality.* Even when our place in the *transcendent* and the *immanent* is secure, bridging continues. Like the eternal moment, our practice is endless.

RELATIONSHIPS ARE
MADE IN HEAVEN

AN OLD SAYING GOES, "Our relationship was made in heaven." Of course, that describes a relationship when everything goes smoothly. Let me say this clearly: *All relationships are made in heaven*—regardless of the strife, turmoil, or discord they entail. The only way to heaven (to our true self, our ground of existence) is through everyday life. As Joko Beck pointed, "Each moment, Life as it is: the only teacher."[17] This life has been given to us so that we can realize our true selves. Each moment is our only opportunity to be on our way. Relationships provide us with such opportunities. So each relationship, just as it is, is necessary.

---

17. Joko Beck, *Nothing Special*, p. 275.

As we've seen, the I-system separates us from our Source, and this separation creates an enormous void. To compensate for this void, the I-system reaches out to another person in hopes that she will fulfill its requirements. So our wishes and beliefs are temporarily fulfilled, bringing periods of bliss. However, with time, the honeymoon ends.

The same beliefs that fired the relationship's attraction sow the seeds for its possible demise. Our I-system intimately interacts with our mate's I-system, and mutual disappointments are inevitable. But these very disappointments are the only road to finding our true selves. With each relationship, unconscious strategies, requirements, core beliefs, and basic fictions come screaming to the surface, pleading for the light of awareness. When the inevitable tension and thoughts of helplessness, frustration, disappointment, and agony come to the forefront, *we have a choice.* We can use the products of our I-system to practice bridging and quietly become aware of the mental and physical components that entails, or we can blame our mate and take out our frustration on him. We have the choice of letting our mate become our best teacher or making him a demon. Of course, choosing the latter leads to the relationship's end and a loss of opportunities.

Here's a striking irony: Often, we are attracted to people who not only have the potential to satisfy some of our I-system's requirements but also ring all the system's alarms. We generally view the former as good and the latter as bad, because it makes us feel vulnerable. Can we face the fact that the ability to be frustrated is a far greater gift than that of satisfying our I-system? Satisfying the system continues the fiction. Frustrating it directs us to the pathway of truth. Our I-system's fiction prevent us from *seeing* the truth. Every single relationship in life has this dual potential: Each can bring us closer to *seeing* the truth or pull us further away by maintaining our fiction.

Even in phases of the relationship when there is harmony, the truth is available if we are mindful of how the I-system successfully fulfills its requirements. However, this is exactly the time when it's most difficult to *experience,* because no anxiety alarms are ringing. When its requirements are being met, the I-system has a tighter grip on us. When things are going smoothly, we believe we are doing well, and this reinforces the entire system. Satisfaction enhances our thinking and positive sensations. Being immersed in these sensations narrows the scope of our awareness. As our circle of awareness contracts, we become more identified with our I-system's requirements, core beliefs, and basic fiction—our *I.* At the beginning of our bridging practice, it is more difficult to *see* the truth, especially when the I-system is humming along nicely. But, regardless of how immersed we become in positive thoughts, bridging is the simple act of returning to the experiences of this very moment.

In everyday usage, the word love is used to describe our attraction to another person (I love you) or the state of a relationship (I'm in love with you). The person being loved gets included in our I-system and interwoven with requirements and strategy. Sometimes, the measure of love is what we would do for our beloved. "I would do this for you."

"I would give up that for you." "I will change for you." Or, finally, "I would die for you." But these are not true measures, because these sacrifices are not altruistic. We make them for our *I*. Altruistic-appearing behavior is always embedded in the fulfillment of our I-system's requirements. This is illustrated in Figure 7, wherein all the lines emanate from the *I*, representing activities directed toward the other, and then return to the *I* to fulfill the system's requirements. As the I-system is reduced, its requirements are lessened, so giving without a need for return becomes possible. We can go further, of course. With continued bridging, we have more access to our Source. We are more fulfilled and so the system requirements are less demanding. Our activities become directed toward all existence—toward life in each moment. But always, there is still a separate *I,* indicating that much of the outpouring continues to be dualistic (see Figure 8, page 64).

When the I-system melts down, we have an outpouring of our life force (as shown in Figure 9, p. 65). With a resting I-system, there is no separate *I* or *you.* There is only *love* realized by an *I* that's not fettered by a belief in separateness, a *you* that is not perceived as an object, and the *universe.* The outpouring of the *limitless I* toward a *limitless you* is *love.* Working, washing dishes, kissing, and hugging—all are equally *love* created anew in each moment by the Creator.

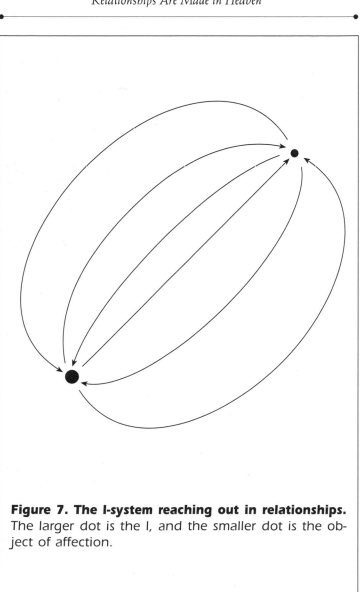

Figure 7. The I-system reaching out in relationships.
The larger dot is the I, and the smaller dot is the object of affection.

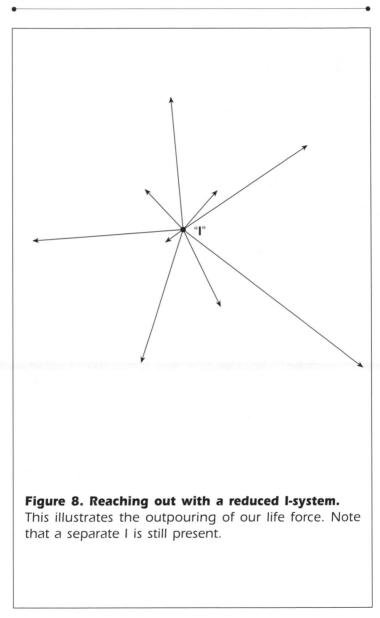

Figure 8. Reaching out with a reduced I-system.
This illustrates the outpouring of our life force. Note
that a separate I is still present.

Figure 9. True love.
Here, there is not a separate subject, no separate object—only love.

I-SYSTEM SEX

SEXUAL URGES ARE thoughts and the sensations located in areas such as the penis, vagina, clitoris, breasts, mouth, anus, and so on. Pleasurable sensations arouse sexual thoughts, and sexual thoughts enhance pleasurable sensations. The I-system incorporates sexual thoughts as well as other thoughts that give rise to pleasant sensations. Thoughts and body sensations that attract awareness are critical to the I-system.

We seek after objects that arouse pleasurable sensations or satisfy I-system while ignoring others. For example, when we behold a crowd of faces, we focus only on the one that fulfills an I-system requirement; the others disappear into a blurred background. In this way, the world is polarized and our senses become tools for the I-system. The ways we walk, talk, and move are influenced by the system's requirements. Actions and facial expressions that get us pleasure or attention from others are favored by the system. Our very thinking is dominated by the system's requirements. Even our smoothly running biological system, which lives by reacting to the circumstances of each moment, is contaminated by the I-system.

The pleasurable sensations of our body functions are just that—no more, no less. Body–mind functioning is simply that: the body and the mind functioning. All of the body functions associated with pleasure become integral to the I-system requirements. The system then takes these over and amplifies the thoughts and associated functions into I-system sexuality. Thus, the I-system takes biological functions, adds on its mission of separation and its requirements, and converts *sex* into I-system sex. The biological system loses its prime role in sexuality as the I-system becomes the controlling factor. So sexual encounters becomes two I-systems seeking individual gratification of their own requirements rather than two body–minds mutually sharing. We are biologically hardwired for *sex*, but the I-system inevitably inserts its program of separation and tries to run the show.

For couples who want to enhance their intimacy, being aware of the I-system's impact on their relationship is an important start. The I-system can treat our mates only as objects. But by bridging, observing and experiencing the system's effects again and again—we can see first-hand how the I-system's requirements are being fulfilled. Every such requirement is based on a separate *I,* which always interferes with mutuality. But as our awareness expands, we can express more of our sexual activity without filtering it through the I-system. Bridging the I-system converts I-system sex into *sex*. With bridging, there is no separate *I* or *you* having to satisfy an individual requirement. There is only the mutual outpouring of our *life force* being experienced. Only bridging to the *divine* allows us to experience the unified functioning of our body–mind. Simultaneously, an unlimited *I* kisses an unlimited *you* and the *divine* kisses the *divine*.

WISDOM

FIRST, LET ME GIVE a definition: Knowing and expressing truth make up *wisdom*. Usually knowing is intepreted in a relative and a conceptual way. The underlying assumption of my I-system is that both *I* and my object of knowing are separate, unchanging, and self-subsistent—that is, that they can exist independently. Once the subject and the object are separated, knowing is dualistic, changing, and always in doubt. The I-system hinders our knowing by keeping us from being present in the moment and preventing our awareness from expanding. On the other hand, in *absolute knowing* we don't divide reality into subject and object—knowing is always present, so there is no doubt. So, seeing truth with the entire *body–mind–universe* is absolute knowing, and this is essential for wisdom.

Wisdom has to do with decision making, judgment, and discernment—that is, with functions of the mind. One prerequisite for decision making is impartiality. Yet the I-system is notorious for wanting to enhance itself by favoring one of the alternatives in a decision. For example, say your child asks you for advice about which college to attend. Immediately, your I-system gets involved, slanting your advice toward or against your own alma mater rather than tuning into what is best for your child. Alternatively, your I-system becomes so preoccupied with being an objective parent that you can't access emotions that would aid in good decision-making. The I-system always exerts pressure on us to make decisions that fulfill its requirements. But where the I-system depends on its subjectivity and partiality, *wisdom* unifies both subject and object with the whole world, leaving no room for partiality. Decision making is then based on an impartial assessment of all information.

Let's take a further look at how information relates to wisdom. Gregory Bateson offered a simple definition of information: "The difference that makes a difference."[18] To clarify what Bateson meant, let me use an example:

> A long time ago, I saw a chicken that could distinguish colors to get food. How could we train a hypothetical chicken, Henri, to distinguish colors? First, we place Henri in a special feeding pen

18. Gregory Bateson, *Steps to an Ecology of Mind: Collected Essays in Anthropology, Psychiatry, Evolution, and Epistemology* (Chicago: University of Chicago Press, 2000).

for one hour each day. Henri receives no food except what he can eat in the pen. In the pen are four different levers, each with a separate color. Blue is 1, red is 2, green is 3, and yellow is 4. All of the grain comes down a central chute, but Henri can access the food only by pecking the red lever.

Initially, Henri pecks randomly: 4, 1, 3, 4, 2, 1, 2, 4, 3, and so on. After pecking for an hour, he is still hungry, because his daily ration depends on Henri pecking the right color 100% of the time. Random pecking gets Henri a quarter of his ration, so he is still hungry. Each day his pecks are different but random. He still gets a quarter of his ration. His different pecks don't make a difference.

Finally, however, Henri begins to observe that the red lever (2) is putting food into the chute. So Henri starts to favor lever 2. His pecks look like this: 3, 4, 1, 2, 3, 2, 2, 1, 2, 4, 2.

A week or so later, his pecks look like this: 1, 2, 2, 2, 3, 2, 2, 2, 2, 4, 2, 2, 2.

Finally, Henri's pecks look like this: 2, 2, 2, 2, 2, 2, 2, 2, 2, 2.

Henri has learned to distinguish red from the other colors to get food. We see in the last three series that Henri's pecks are different, and it makes a difference. He receives about half of his ration on the first series, more than three-quarters on the second series, and 100% on the third series.

The difference that makes a difference is information. Henri uses the same energy each day, his series is different each day—the difference is that, with the last three series, Henri has begun to process information.

Information is stored in our brain cells and in other cells throughout our bodies. For example, the DNA in a fertilized human egg contains all the information necessary to create a complete person, yet it is so small that hundreds of eggs would fit on the head of a pin. The information needed to create all 100 U.S. senators would have ample room to dance all night on the head of a pin. Even inanimate objects, such as a speck of dust, contain billions of bits of information. To have form or substance requires order, information. You might think that empty space, a vacuum, contains no information. But, as Stephen Hawkings pointed out, our "empty space" is actually full of pairs of opposite particles—and occasionally some will "jump out."[19] Thus, emptiness contains information; it does not depend on space and time. Information exists in the moment, where there is no duration, no beginning or end. It does not have material characteristics and so exists throughout all of space and time. The physical universe is the momentary realization of universal information. The Source of all creation is devoid of material characteristics, yet contains all the information necessary for the universe's creation.

The difference that makes a difference in the material

19. Stephen Hawking, *A Brief History of Time.*

realm of *reality* is Henri pecking differently to get food. If Henri does not process information, he gets only a quarter of his daily ration. In the non material or spiritual realm, the difference that makes a difference is the appearance and disappearance of the material universe in each moment. If information was not processed in the spiritual realm there would be no physical world. Without God, we do not exist. If there is no spiritual realm, there is no material realm; and no universal information means no existence.

It is only through *universal consciousness* that we can fully experience universal information. *I consciousness* is a limited part of *universal consciousness* and has limited access to universal information. *Body–mind consciousness* contains a larger portion of *universal consciousness* and so has larger access. *Wisdom* is related not only to how much information we have stored in our brains but to how much universal intelligence we experience and express in each moment. When the I-system clings to information, our awareness is reduced, shrinking our wisdom. *Wisdom is universal intelligence in action in our everyday lives.* Wisdom means we are in harmony and balance with our Source, so we express the Creator's will.

Bridging our I-system allows subject and object to merge intimately with the universe, allowing wisdom to flow. Without duality—without separation—existence springs from nonexistence. Creation within the moment both explodes and implodes. Think of it this way: Wisdom is mountains standing tall; apples being round, red, and crisp. When our I-system melts, wisdom is expressed in our compassionate actions. The mountain, the apple, and the person with a resting I-system have no choice but to express wisdom within each moment.

SILENCE IS GOLDEN

L IKE MOST THINGS, personal silence has an inner and an outer aspect. Outer silence is simply not talking, being quiet; inner silence is the absence of thought—that is, a quiet mind. In bridging, a quiet mind implies a tranquil mind, one that is not moved by thoughts, sensations, or perceptions. It is a state of *choice-less awareness* with both activity and calmness.

So, let's consider the complete spectrum of silence as it is experienced from *I consciousness* through *body–mind consciousness* to *universal consciousness*.

- Initially, at the level of *I consciousness*, silence is experienced solely as the absence of sound or noise.

- As awareness expands to *body–mind consciousness*,

silence is experienced as a calmness, serenity, or tranquility of the body–mind, which allows the coming and going of thoughts, perceptions, and sensations. This state is associated with a decreasing I-system influence over our awareness and body–mind.

• *Silence* in *universal consciousness* is manifested by an unchanging presence and a continuously changing *presencing* of the manifest world. Without an I-system, there is no duality and so no particular body–mind experience. Serenity and tranquility may or may not be present, but *silence* is always present.

The serenity and tranquility of a quiet mind are quite powerful, because their roots are in *silence*. Silence is the golden pathway to our Source. But the I-system, whose life depends on thinking and contracting awareness, finds silence both incomprehensible and frightening. Remember, the I-system's existence is based on the fiction of separation. The system is its own god, and it doesn't want to be aware of any other god—not even the one God. Silence means that the I-system's self-centered operations lessen; yet we still see, hear, feel, think and act—all with expanded awareness. Thus silence, at any level, presents a golden opportunity for intimacy with God—through prayer, Bible study, religious ritual, solitude in nature, or meditation. Because serenity and tranquility are rooted in *silence*, the support is limitless. A silent night *is* a holy night; a silent moment, a holy moment. It is holy because creation is born from *silence*. The more intimate we are with silence, the more whole and holy we are. But we can experience silence only in the present moment. So, bridging entails coming back again and again to find our silent and holy moment.

FEAR IS THE I-SYSTEM'S BACKBONE

F EAR (OR ANXIETY[20]) is a combination of fearful thoughts and bodily sensations. We're all familiar with the fight-or-flight reaction. When faced with a situation we see as dangerous, our body sends an alarm and prepares us to flee or fight. Adrenaline is released throughout the body, increasing our heart and respiration rates and preparing the body–mind for a response.

Freud noted that our mind uses just a small signal of anxiety to warn us of pending danger.[21] Anxiety then

---

20. Sometimes we use fear and anxiety interchangeably; technically, fear is associated with a specific external situation, whereas anxiety is an anticipation of, or a preparation for, a known or unknown dangerous situation.
21. Sigmund Freud, "Inhibitions, Symptoms, and Anxiety," in *Standard Edition of the Complete Works of Sigmund Freud* , Volume XX, p. 1926.

mobilizes the functions of the mind to deal with the situation. Thinking, planning, acting, problem solving, reality testing, alertness, and so on are brought into play to deal with the danger. If these activities are successful, we avoid a full-fledged fight-or-flight reaction.

In contrast to our biological system, which uses fear and anxiety to manage its environment, the I-system uses the entire spectrum of fears and anxieties to accomplish its mission of separation. In fact, the backbone of the I-system is fear. This fear captures our attention, and we become servants to the system. Rather than being adaptive tools, fear and anxiety become instruments of the I-system.

The fear of "losing our identity"—that is, the fear of not existing as separate, unchanging, self-subsistent entities—is quite powerful. Even though we don't really have a separate existence and so have nothing to lose, the I-system's existence is dependent on maintaining this fiction. Losing that identity is death to the system. So to preserve itself, the I-system sends an alarm to every part of our body–mind. Before the system sounds a full alarm, we feel gradually increasing signals that cause mental and physical activity aimed at correcting the dreaded situation. For example, a friend recently shared with me an incident that occurred while she was playing the organ. She suddenly experienced her fingers playing by themselves. As the playing continued, she became frightened that "she" was not playing the music. Although the music was wonderful, she was afraid of losing herself. To control her fear, she began to think and try hard, and eventually she gained control over her fingers. When I asked her, "Who do you think was playing the organ?" she intuitively responded, "My soul."

Another example of this fear is subtle and often goes unnoticed. During peaceful, calm, and tranquil periods, the spaces between our thoughts lengthen as we become relaxed. You may be looking at a sunset and experiencing oneness with nature. Suddenly, your mind is filled with thoughts such as, "This is the best sunset I've ever seen. How long will it last? Without that cloud bank, the colors would be even more vivid." Your harmony, unity, and balance with nature are lost. The I-system rushes in to preserve its identity as a separate *I*. Unaware of the I-system's fear, all you experience is the influx of thoughts. If you had returned your awareness to the moment present at that time, you would have sensed your body tensing.

The I-system has us convinced that its self-conception is our true identity. It even tries to fool us into believing there is an entity within us that is separate, unchanging, and self-subsistent—one that lives on after we die. But our true identity springs forth as our I-system is bridged rather than believed. Who we are rests in God's hands, not in those of our I-system.

Let me briefly touch upon emergency fears here—the fears caused by fire, earthquakes, car accidents, unprovoked assault, rape, shootings, war, and the like. In life-and-death situations, it is our biological system that handles emergency responses. Often, people report that during an emergency they act quickly, calmly, and effectively. An emergency puts us square in the moment, where our I-system cannot function. It expands our awareness, brings us to our senses, and gives us strength we can't even imagine. The thinking in an emergency is functional. Our cognitive and body functions are temporarily freed of the I-system and function optimally. Without self-centered thinking, being in the moment is natural. It's only after the emergency is over that the tension of the I-system sets in.

It is this feeling of *total aliveness*—when awareness expands through our *body–mind consciousness*—that causes some of us to be attracted to dangerous situations. But no matter how many dangerous situations we experience, the I-system does not lessen. In fact, the system is fed by dangerous situations. Thus, danger-seeking behavior becomes part of the I-system. At first glance, it seems that periods of "forced expanded awareness" should be helpful; but, in reality, they serve only to contract everyday awareness because they add intensity to the I-system. Even professional athletes who get "into the zone" and experience expanded awareness and decreased I-system function during competition have the same problem when events end. Success feeds the I-system.

Addictions (chemical, alcohol, and others) are terror-driven I-systems that function to reduce fear at the expense of the body–mind. This attempt results in severe impairment to the hormone, polypeptide, and neurotransmitter systems. With these impairments, expanding awareness through *body–mind consciousness* is difficult. However, returning again and again to the present moment is an effective practice. Bridging offers new opportunities in the addiction field.

Now let's look at some other fears: Miscellaneous fears

not associated with acute emergency situations are composed of a mental component (fearful thoughts) and a bodily component (tension and malfunctioning of organs and systems). Examples include fears of poverty, loss of job or prestige, school failure, failure in an activity, loss of a loved one, illness, old age, death, phobias, free-floating fears, fear of losing impulse control, fear of not living up to inner demands, embarrassment, and shame. All of these fearful emotions—whether we refer to them as fear, anxiety, depression, guilt, or shame—are similar. Even though the fear is related to an external situation, it becomes enmeshed in the I-system's agenda of fulfilling requirements rather than responding to the external situation.

So fear is the backbone of the I-system. It is the system's signal that one of its requirements is in jeopardy of not being fulfilled. For example, fears associated with job loss are not simply results of real factors related to being out of work; instead, they are related to a violation of the I-system requirement of always having a good job. Our deep-seated fears and tensions arise because we experience them as life-or-death situations for the limited *I*. Thus, our anxiety alarm sounds as if we're facing immediate assault. Our thoughts and tensions are more appropriate for fighting a saber-tooth tiger than for finding a new job. And our fearful thoughts, tensions, and attempts at avoidance impair our ability to deal with significant events in life.

The fears I am discussing here are the feelings of uneasiness and anxiety caused solely by the I-system's attempt to preserve itself. They cannot be eliminated by self-help endeavors. Indeed, self-help methods only strengthen the I-system and prevent us from experiencing expanding awareness and finding our ground of existence. It is only in the ground of existence that we find peace of mind, joy, and wisdom for dealing with life's situations.

TRAUMA AND
VISCERAL HELPLESSNESS

CONSIDER A MAN WITH a heart condition who is shoveling snow. The effort causes his heart muscles to work harder, increasing the demand for blood flow. When the blood flow is insufficient, the heart muscles begin to malfunction, which further reduces the blood flow. If the blood flow is not restored, heart muscles begin to die. After such a trauma, the heart functions less efficiently, and the man can't do the same physical work he used to. Trauma occurs when an event drives essential variables outside of their usual limits, creating new patterns of body function and behavior. If the body's coping mechanisms had restored adequate blood flow to the heart before these changes took place, the snow shoveling event would not be classified as a trauma.

The horrifying events of September 11, 2001, challenged the coping mechanisms of all the survivors. Essential variables of the body–mind were driven to their limits and beyond. After the attack, many survivors demonstrated symptoms of trauma, including intrusive memories, hyperarousal and hypervigilance, sleeplessness, bad dreams, episodes of sweating, palpitations, and tension. These are normal reactions to trauma. Victims of a trauma often show alterations of behavior, brain function, neurotransmitters, and hormones that were not previously present.[22]

Trauma challenges a person's usual coping mechanism. Depending on the person and the nature of the event, a trauma can lead to maladaptive changes (as illustrated above) or to adaptive changes. For example, allowing a child to experience age-appropriate delays in gratification challenges her to develop new behaviors. Although she may react with temper tantrums and experience a trauma, she learns from the "stretching" experience and, with time and love, learns new behaviors.

All systems can be overwhelmed by traumatic events. Then body-mind functions that are essential for survival are jeopardized. We experience this ultimate threat as a visceral helplessness, characterized by a massive outpouring of sensory-motor activity, progressively fragmented and

---

22. S. M. Southwick, R. Yehuda, and D. S. Charney, "Neurobiological Alternations in PTSD: Review of the Clinical Literature." In C. S. Fullerton and R. J. Ursano (eds.), *Post-Traumatic Stress Disorders: Acute and Long-Term Responses to Trauma and Disaster* (pp 241–266). Washington, DC: American Psychiatric Press, 1991.

disorganized thoughts, and compromised states of consciousness. At the onset, the system generates increasingly stronger anxiety signals to warn of the impending danger. These signals are less intense than the full reaction and mobilize the system's resources to defend against pending trauma. When I-system requirements are progressively unfilled, even though our biological system is not externally threatened, the I-system becomes overwhelmed. It then uses the biological system as a pawn, as the entire body–mind becomes impaired by sweating, tenseness, shortness of breath, palpitations, agitation, fearful and helpless thoughts.

A child's I-system cannot tolerate being overwhelmed. Children structure their core beliefs and requirements to defend against the experience of visceral helplessness. For example, a child with a core belief that, "I'm good and deserve pleasure," and a requirement of, "The world will be good to me," will experience visceral helplessness if he is subjected to physical abuse. As the abuse continues, his I-system changes its core belief to, "I'm bad and deserve to suffer," which protects the child against repeated experiences of visceral helplessness. If abuse occurs again, the child's I-system now has a sense of mastery because it believes it *caused* the abuse, rather than being a helpless, passive victim. Requirements begin evolving to fulfill the new core belief. The child may even develop requirements to suffer further abuse. If the abuse continues, it will not cause visceral helplessness because the new requirement won't be violated. As he grows up, his I-system may develop requirements of self-abuse or of abusing others, which unconsciously confirms his core belief of his own badness and need to suffer. Thus, the I-system remains active, in control, and removed from the experience of visceral helplessness. Later in life seemingly adaptive requirements such as "I'll work hard and be successful to prove I'm good," are still related to the core belief: "I'm bad." These eventually lead to patterns of suffering in spite of mountains of success. Illness, accidents, even minor random misfortunes are used to confirm the core belief.

On the other hand, a child whose parents have good parenting skills might have a core belief of, "The world will satisfy all my needs." This core belief sets the stage for repeated trauma to the I-system, even with ideal parenting, because the core belief is impossible to fulfill. Thus, when the child's need isn't immediately fulfilled, she experiences this as a traumatic event. Eventually, an overwhelming situation develops as the whole biological system participates. Repeated frustrations lead to new requirements such as, "I'm the only one who can take care of myself." This is the I-system's attempt to stay in control. The I-system experiences all events as self-centered. Thus, if the child gets sick, the requirement of taking care of herself is violated and the "I-system" reacts as if it is facing a traumatic event. No matter what the I-system's structure of core beliefs, it always experiences being overwhelmed when its requirements are not met, even if there is absolutely no threat to one's well-being. Whenever we experience visceral helplessness, our I-system, fearing annihilation, mobilizes body–mind activities to defend against the threat.

So, we see how various forms of trauma continue to

shape the I-system. Trauma not only energizes require-ments of living the past, but also causes the system to gen-erate a new requirement of *dyspresence*; a need to avoid being present in the moment. Bridging the I-system weak-ens this requirement by returning again and again to ex-perience the present moment, which expands awareness and offers us new choices and freedoms. Resting in the moment, we do not have to fix or alter the past. Instead, we come to experience the limitless support of our Source. The testimonials of thousands of members of Alcoholics Anonymous—who have a spiritual experience in which they acknowledge their own helplessness along with an ex-perience of a "Power greater than myself"—supports this premise.

AGGRESSION

A GGRESSION HAS BEEN part of the human experience since our earliest history. It has perplexed theologians, biologists, anthropologists, philosophers, sociologists, psychologists, psychiatrists, and psychoanalysts alike. Experts are still divided about whether we have a primary aggressive drive or whether aggression is always a reaction to an experience of injury. But they do agree that aggression is pervasive in humans, not only in overt behaviors and competition but also in fueling physical activities such as running or tossing a ball. For our purposes, aggression consists of angry, controlling, dominating, violent thoughts, along with their body's activities.

The survival benefit of strong aggressive drives is self-evident. An animal's aggressive drives not only protects it against threats to its safety, but allows the strongest to survive and propagate. Our biological system does the same; however, the I-system has a far different agenda. The I-system's mission is to preserve and protect our conception of a separate and limited *I*. This mission, rather than biological drives, is responsible for human aggression.

In contrast to the biological system, which cannot ignore reality, the I-system depends on spinning thoughts rather than external reality. In fact, it can spin almost any type of event into a major insult—and, once the spinning starts, fear and anxiety increase dramatically, causing tension and agitation. As the spin increases, our awareness contracts. We experience ourselves as closed off, empty, and suffering. Then we blame whoever was associated with the initial event for our inner turmoil. When your body is full of tension and your mind full of vengeful thoughts, it's very likely your behavior will be aggressive, especially when you have a target. So we see that violent behavior is dependant on the I-system.

The *I* at the center of your I-system includes not just your body–mind but also your clothing, possessions, prestige, knowledge, pride, weapons, family, clan, country, race, religion, soul, conception of God, sports team, political party, social issues, and on and on. The system treats these *I-aggregates* in much the same way it does the *I*. Your synthetic functioning blends this strange and ever-changing concoction of "you" into a unit—the *aggregate-I*—and generates requirements for it. These requirements might be, "No one will call me names," "No one will insult my family," "No one should appear strange to me," "No one will oppose my beliefs or my activities," "No one will speak against my country or religion," and so on. When these requirements are breached, even if there is no threat to your safety or welfare, your I-system is activated.

The *aggregate-I* is the link between the individual I-system and the collective I-system[23] and helps us understand the aggressive behavior of groups. Each person in the group has at least one *aggregate-I* with related requirements in common. These may involve politics, race, religion, sports—the list is almost endless. The functioning of society reflects its collective I-system. For example, in Nazi Germany, the *aggregate-I* included Germany and the "German race." The requirements were these:

1. No one should challenge the superiority of Germany.

2. Germany should conquer the world.

3. Inferior races and people must be eliminated.

When a resonance happens among the individual I-systems, a collective I-system forms. This resonance then feeds back to enhance the individual I-systems. The more we experience ourselves as separate, either individually or as a group, the more threatened we feel, because the I-system's backbone is fear. This vicious cycle can lead inevitably to individual or group violence.

---

23. I discuss the collective I-system more fully on pp. 115-120.

CONTROL

A s HUMANS, WE WANT to control our own health care, our financial futures, our bodies, our minds, our destinies. The very idea that someone else is controlling us raises our hackles. My first thought about living in a dictatorship is, "Someone is controlling my life." The more we believe we are being controlled, the more rebellious we feel. We abhor being controlled. Yet the I-system is controlling us without mercy and we don't raise a finger, because we don't even see it.

The I-system cannot function without control. It tries to control all our thinking so that thoughts which threaten its core belief or requirements do not occur. When they do arise, the system sounds an alarm, prompting a response. It may repress or deny the fearful thought, avoid the external precipitant of the thought, or create a diversion (for example, psychosomatic symptoms or a personal drama). Because the system rejects a thought such as "I may lose my job" by limiting our awareness, we pass over any opportunity to expand our awareness to evaluate and enhance our job performance.

Remember, the I-system incessantly attempts to control the body-mind and the outer world by fulfilling its requirements. These controlling activities are not responses to real challenges to our health or welfare, but they are based solely on I-system functioning. So, everyday situations—a friend ignoring us, the stock market falling, not getting a raise, having a cold, waiting in line, feeling tired, not having sex—generate anxiety and tension because they violate the I-system's requirements. This system controls our lives more than a maximum-security prison.

The I-system has a desired outcome for almost every situation. When this outcome is not forthcoming, the system activates our anxiety network and hampers our body–mind in its adaptive activities. To see how futile the I-system's activities are, let's look at Murphy's Law: If something can go wrong, it will go wrong. Stephen Hawking makes the interesting observation that Murphy's Law is related to entropy (or chaos).[24] In nature, entropy always increases—that is, all systems become more disorganized over time. Because there are always more disorganized than organized states, Murphy's Law is likely because what we want to happen is one state but what **can** happen is one

---

24. Hawking, *A Brief History of Time.*

of numerous states. So, to ensure a desired outcome, the I-system must be constantly tense and busy.

Entropy keeps the I-system constantly on guard. No matter what strategy the system adopts to ensure successful outcomes, eventually and inevitably it will fall short. Even perfectionism and obsessive-compulsive strategies fail. This failure gives rise to the "fix it" strategy. We all see our share of this strategy. The I-system fixes the world and itself for the sole purpose of fulfilling its requirement, so it can maintain its fiction of separation. But this fix it approach will always be fruitless, and the I-system strengthens as we constantly try to make things perfect. Even if a strategy seems to succeed and we get rich and famous, the system is never satisfied. It is based on a fiction; so our success never brings peace of mind, because our I-system is based on fear and tension.

But our body–mind knows we are not broken and so we don't need to be fixed. Its functioning is dictated by what we need for life in each moment. Walking, playing, fixing a flat tire, taking an aspirin, planning, deciding to eat—these are the natural activities of the body–mind. It functions in harmony and balance with life as it is in each moment.

We can't outthink the I-system. Trying to control the system or make it our enemy—being angry at it, hating it, thinking about getting rid of it—only strengthens it, because all those thoughts against the I-system become part of the I-system.

Furthermore, trying to destroy the system reduces our chances to experience our true selves, because **every part**

of the body–mind, particularly the I-system, is a blessing. If gravity did not pull us down, how would we know the way to heaven? The I-system simultaneously pulls us away from and leads us back our true selves. The structure and functioning of your particular I-system is totally unique. So there can be no standard guide or cookbook to show you the way—your way. Instead, bridging the I-system means being mindful of your I-system's activities during your everyday life and returning again and again to being present in the moment. Watching its almost endless varieties of controlling activities weakens its iron grip and expands your consciousness toward heaven.

PAIN

PAIN IS AN INHERENT PART of the human condition.
Sooner or later, we all suffer pain. Let's watch the I-system's
role in a painful situation—say, a heavy board falling on my
foot. Without the I-system's involvement, I reflexively
withdraw the foot. If the damage appears severe, I go to
the emergency room. After an examination and treatment,
I follow my doctor's instructions. It's plain and simple. But
soon, my I-system becomes involved with thoughts like,
"How could I be stupid enough to let a board fall on my
foot? That board shouldn't have been there in the first
place. These things always happen to me. How can I work
if I can't walk? When will it stop hurting?" These spinning
thoughts of "poor me" enhance my I-system, causing anxiety and tension. Experiencing pain also violates an I-system requirement, which then generates thoughts about

fighting the pain. This I-system activity restricts my aware-ness, which enhances my pain. The longer the pain con-tinues, the greater the involvement of my I-system—un-til, eventually, my whole personality becomes reorganized around my pain.

But pain can be a stimulus to awareness, so it can ac-tually help in bridging. Remember, bridging is expanding our awareness from *I consciousness* through *body–mind con-sciousness* to *universal consciousness*. So, pain can help us expand our consciousness and healing, or it can become embedded in the I-system, resulting in chronic pain anxi-ety and restricted awareness. We always have a choice, ei-ther to use the physical pain to heighten our awareness and facilitate bridging, or to allow the I-system to go into high gear with "Why me?" thoughts. The central issue in heal-ing is what our awareness does. Expanding our awareness opens our gateway to the Source and enhances healing. Restricted awareness leads to tension and morbidity.

Bridging is a non-selective awareness of our thoughts, sounds, sights, and body sensations. With this awareness, we can simultaneously experience the pain *and* the sensation of our breathing, the pattern of the rug, traffic sounds, and even thoughts like, "Why me?" The larger the circumfer-ence of our awareness, the more we will be aware of all the changing sensations we had labeled as pain. By not pushing away the sensations or enhancing them, we allow them to change in quality and quantity, and even to come and go. With pain we have a challenge: We can satisfy the requirements of the I-system and reinforce its fictional basis or we can satisfy our desire to *see* the truth and let our consciousness expand. Pain gives us the opportunity to be present in the moment, expand our awareness, and enhance our healing.

Because it involves the entire I-system and personality, chronic pain is a difficult problem. However, the practice is same: choice-less awareness of all mental and physical sensations simultaneously. Bridging is not pushing away or enhancing thoughts or sensations. Some people find that focusing their awareness on other things is helpful—for example, visualizing a sunny beach or mountaintop, having pleasant memories, thinking of "other problems," or focusing strict attention on breathing. This may help you to briefly settle your mind, but if you use this technique exclusively, you limit your ability to expand your awareness. This narrow focus means you are actively pushing away unwanted thoughts and sensations. But these thoughts and sensations are then energized and will come back later with a vengeance. With an all-inclusive non-focused awareness, our thoughts and sensations are free to come and go. They change in each moment, and so our healing is enhanced.

Labeling thoughts such as, "I am having the thought that the pain will never go away, " "I am having the thought that bridging will not help me," allows us to become less identified with our I-system and expands our consciousness. When the mind is very active, labeling is helpful. Always remember that the goal "to get rid of the pain" is just a thought, which will enhance our I-system. We should continue to return to the present moment with awareness of all our body–mind sensations, moment by moment. Expanding our awareness has many physical, mental, and spiritual benefits.

You may find that pain or disease that has not responded to conventional or holistic medicine is helped by bridging. Healing has both a knowable and an unknowable aspect. The former is the direct result of diminishing I-system. Once the pain or diseased state is embedded in the I-system, it fulfills the I-system's agenda rather than the body's mission of healing. The component of the pain that is embedded in the I-system will tend to heal with bridging. Remember, I-system functioning is always associated with fear and body tension that impedes healing. The unknowable aspect, on the other hand, we cannot grasp with our rational mind. It results from the expansion of our consciousness and the subsequent freeing of the inflow from our Source. There are many practices (including choice-less awareness) that expand consciousness and decrease the I-system. Being in the moment always expands awareness and creates space for healing. Miracle healing clearly results from consciousness expanding to our Source. Whatever practice enhances this intimacy with our Source increases the probability of healing. If miracle healing takes place, of course, the I-system stands ready and waiting to take over and embed whatever happens into itself. If this occurs and the I-system puffs up with pride, we simply return again to bridging and reuniting with our Source.

BEYOND THE PLEASURE PRINCIPLE

A N INFANT'S BEHAVIOR OF seeking immediate gratification is motivated by the Pleasure Principle. On the
other hand, the adult behavior of delaying and working
toward gratification when immediate fulfillment is impossible is motivated by the Reality Principle. When a chroni-
cally homeless man stays on the streets drinking himself to
death, we wonder what drives him to such a terrible end.
Criminals repeat the same crimes over and over again.
Smokers with lung cancer keep smoking cigarettes. Addictions to drugs, alcohol, and gambling; repeated, painful
dreams—what drives behaviors that are not pleasurable?

Eighty years ago, in his classic work *Beyond the Pleasure
Principle*, Freud attempted to answer the question, "Why do

we continue to repeat behaviors which are painful, unpleasant, or even traumatic?"[25] He put forward a controversial "death instinct" that is held in balance by the life instinct. Freud believed this death instinct accounted for behaviors that contradict the body's natural inclination for pleasure and adaptation. He also suggested that repeated painful dreams and some compulsive behaviors can be accounted for by the Pleasure Principle, because their activities reduce the pressure of an unconscious need for punishment (guilt). Thus, these dreams and behaviors might still be motivated by pleasure—the pleasure of guilt reduction.

Today, system theory lets us understand driven, self-destructive behavior in a much simpler way: The I-system is driven by its mission to fulfill its core beliefs and requirements. Whether the requirement is "keeping myself healthy by eating well and exercising daily" or "drinking myself numb daily," the system functions in exactly the same way by forcing the body–mind to fulfill its core belief and requirement. So, until the I-system is bridged, *all* behaviors are driven by its core belief and requirements. In the first case, not exercising or eating well would cause anxiety, which would prompt remedial action. In the second case, not drinking daily would cause anxiety and tension until the person takes a drink. The I-system uses all of its resources to find ways of fulfilling its requirements, regardless of the outcome to our body–mind. Thus, the I-system

---

25. Sigmund Freud, "Beyond the Pleasure Principle," in *Standard Edition of the Complete Works of Sigmund Freud* (Vol. XVIII, pp. 1–66).

always operates beyond the Pleasure Principle. It does not seek pleasure or gains for the body–mind, it only seeks fulfillment of its core belief, to secure the existence of the limited *I*. Even if the requirements seem positive to us, the I-system can't quit creating tension and anxiety—unless and until bridging occurs.

Many of us will find it hard to believe that the I-system, a subsystem of the biological system, has engineered a coup, demonstrating this much power over the entire biological system. Are there other biological examples? Well, cancer cells are a subsystem of the biological system that have engineered a coup and have taken control of the whole system. Their mission is to propagate their own cells, and that mission subverts the body's mission of preserving life.

To better understand the drive to self-destructive activity, remember how systems work. A system is a set of variables, like blood pressure, pulse, temperature, and blood sugar. The system functions to keep the variables within certain limits. For example, our biological system attempts to keep our temperature between 97 and 99 degrees. When that requirement is breached, certain body functions are activated to increase or decrease the temperature. All the system knows is to fulfill its mission and keep the variables within certain limits. Just as a guided missile fulfills its mission by hitting a target, our biological system fulfills its mission by preserving our life and the life of our species. The I-system, a subsystem of the biological system, fulfills its mission by preserving its basic fiction and core beliefs. Once the requirements for the core belief are in place, the I-system uses all of its resources to accomplish its mission.

Most of us don't even know we have an I-system, let alone its requirements. Like a guided missile, we are driven toward a target. A requirement could be using all of our resources to stay healthy, or it could be using all of our resources to be miserable. What makes the situation even more tragic is that, even if we are fortunate enough to have a pleasant set of requirements, the mission of the I-system is solely to preserve the separate *I*. So if the I-system is successful, we lose our ability to reunite with our Source and have true peace of mind.

Before we begin bridging the I-system, all of its requirements are automatically being fulfilled. For example, take the requirement "I need to suffer." In our rational minds, we are absolutely certain we don't want to suffer; however, we wonder why bad things always happen to us. On the other hand, with the requirement "I need to be successful," we wonder why we can't relax or enjoy life and peace of mind after securing our goals. The I-system continually creates tension and anxiety to perpetuate its existence. Bridging the I-system expands our awareness of its requirements, strategy, core beliefs, personality, and so on. With continuing bridging, we become less identified with the system's mission of fulfilling requirements and preserving the limited *I*. We then have a choice of fulfilling our I-system's requirements or being fulfilled by our true self with God.

DEPRESSION

DEPRESSION HAS BIOLOGICAL, psychological, and social aspects. In this chapter, we will focus on the I-system's role in the range of depressions, from transient, everyday feelings of being burdened by life to clinical, life-endangering states.[26]

The I-system places a heavy burden on us by insisting we fulfill its requirements day and night. In addition to the system's demands for fulfillment, there is raw suffering in each and every cell of our body–mind because of the I-system's constant effort to separate us from our Source. Our life becomes suffering, not because of our existence, but because of the I-system. Let me give some examples

---

26. Bridging techniques are not recommended for clinical depressions or mental disorders. Professional help is recommended.

of the heavy burden that our own I-system creates for us.

Sometimes we wake up dreading the day. Life seems a burden. Day-to-day existence is hard. Our bodies are heavy and our minds filled with sad thoughts. Our interest is withdrawn from the world. This slowing of mental and physical function is a sign that the body–mind is wilting under the pressures of the I-system. As the pressure of the system mounts, the biological system becomes less and less effective. The I-system superimposes its mission of separation on the body's mission of preserving life. Fulfilling a core belief, such as "The world won't fulfill my needs because I'm not good enough" leads to requirements such as, "I deserve to suffer." Then, to fulfill these requirements, the I-system uses its ability to create anxiety, tension, and behaviors that promote suffering. No matter how intense our suffering, we are fulfilling the I-system's mission. Eventually, the I-system spawns requirements such as, "I do not deserve to live." Soon, the biological system begins to dysfunction and, in the most severe situation, the I-system commits homicide, killing the biological system. In this case, a successful suicide is as much an I-system victory as making a million dollars. It preserves the separate, unchanging, self-subsistent *I*. In severe depression, the victory of the I-system is accompanied by a surrendering of the biological system. The I-system believes that its *I* lives on, even after death, unchanged, separate, and self-subsistent.

Like other emotions, depression is a particular combination of thoughts and body sensations. In a depressed state, the biological system is surrendering its mission to the I-system. The sad thoughts carry out the I-system's core beliefs and requirements, while the physical sensations are the price our body–mind pays. Depression saps our energy and narrows our awareness, making it difficult to be present in the moment. But bridging is simply being aware of the sad thoughts and weary sensations. Including everyday sensations like traffic sounds, neighbor noise, and gravity expands our awareness and promotes healing.

The I-system flourishes with thoughts of self-hatred. In fact, the thought, "I am a terrible person and should suffer," bolsters the I-system as much as the thought, "I am a great person and entitled to good things." Both of these are products of the I-system's core belief and foster the separate, unchanging, self-subsistent *I*. Sensations like a heavy and painful body tend to make the negative thoughts more believable. When we think, "I'm a bad person," the I-system convinces us that our body is painful because we are bad. It is important to realize that depressive thoughts, especially those that are self-critical and self-punishing, are only thoughts. It is our belief in the thoughts, and not the thoughts per se, which causes the problem. Pushing thoughts away only gives them more energy. Labeling self-critical thoughts tends to lessen our belief in them.

The role of bridging in a depressed state is identical to bridging in all other activities of life: We return again and again to mindfulness of our mental and physical sensations. With expanding awareness, we can experience the changing nature and quality of sad feelings and heavy body sensations. As bridging continues, we come to have less belief in the negative thoughts. As our belief in the negative thoughts lessens, the body relaxes and the biological system gains freedom to return to a more functional state. Our practice continues unchanged, with mindfulness of thoughts, perceptions, and sensations. As bridging continues, the emptiness and suffering of our body–mind can be replaced with the fullness and lightness of our true self. Bridging is our life's everyday work.

THE ORIGIN OF GOOD AND EVIL

To FURTHER OUR UNDERSTANDING of bridging, let's look at two extreme examples of evil behavior. On September 11, 2001, we were shocked, grieved, and devastated by the terrorist attack on America. On April 19, 1995, one of America's sons bombed the Murrah Federal Building in Oklahoma City. We know that bridging opens the gateway to God and gives us responsibility for the resulting flow of goodness in our behavior. But how does this gateway close?

In his written statement before his execution in June 2001, Timothy McVeigh, the convicted Oklahoma City bomber, quoted the last two lines of William Henley's poem "Invictus":

> I am master of my fate;
> I am captain of my soul.

McVeigh was reinforcing his belief that his I-system ruled his destiny. His I-system sealed off his gateway to God. When the limited *I* replaces God, the entire world suffers. Psychology, psychiatry, and psychoanalysis have been unable to include this all-important factor of human behavior in their theories—because they have excluded the spiritual face of *reality*. The world's religions, on the other hand, have clearly understood the importance of God in human behavior.

McVeigh chose to believe his I-system and interpreted the *I* in the poem as referring to his limited and separate *I*. William Henley was probably referring to the unlimited true self that appears with bridging. Rather than being a justification for evil, the poem becomes a commentary on the greatness of the human spirit *as it is released from the bondage of the I-system*. Let me paraphrase the poem's last two lines:

> Being my true self masters my fate;
> My true self in harmony with God captains my soul.

Whether religious or not, whether spiritual or not, or whether moral or not, we all have strong aspirations for bridging, which are fed by our Source. This aspiration is a direct result of the I-system's constant effort to reinforce its basic fiction. Every part of the body–mind cries out in suffering protest. Because all the system can do is try to solidify its fiction, it can never calm the thirsting for re-union. This existential suffering is due to the existence of the I-system. We all have a deep aspiration to see the *truth* of our existence. Bridging is rooted in this *truth*. Finally, our awareness, which is grounded in *consciousness*, naturally expands toward its Source. Only through bridging to God can pure moral behavior result. Opposing these innate aspirations is the I-system. So, our morality is determined by whether we choose to trust our Source or our I-system.

Many of us would conclude that the greater the choice, the better our behavior. We love free will and choice. Free will and our I-system are indivisible. When the I-system melts down, we have total freedom and no free will—that is, no choice. The more intimate we are with God, the less choice we have, because we are doing God's Will. For those blessed individuals who have melted down their I-systems and are living each moment in the *universal consciousness*, each act or behavior has no self-interest and is the only act possible in the moment. They do not *choose* to do God's Will; they have no choice but to do God's Will. Until we reach this stage, we have a choice in each and every moment: We can be present in the moment with *truth*, or we can drift with our I-system. Constantly choosing the latter cannot help but result in behaviors lacking in compassion.

Our old friend, entropy, can shed more light on the role of choice here. Simply stated, entropy is a physical law saying that disorder of a system always increases. In a deck of playing cards that is well shuffled, it is more likely the cards will be in a disordered state because there are so many more disordered states than the one ordered state present when we opened the new deck. It takes a force outside the deck to create this ordered initial state. Only God, as a force outside the I-system, can enable us to reach our original state with God. The I-system on its own cannot create goodness or pure moral behavior.

Both the great saint and the great sinner start out with free choice. Both end up with no choice. The saint has little choice in doing God's Will; the sinner, although believing he has freedom of choice, has little choice in following the dictates of his hypertrophied I-system. The great sinner must create havoc to maintain his ordered state. The great saint's ordered state is in pure harmony and balance with God and all existence. Although behaviors of both are actualizations of our existence, one is perfect bridging of the I-system and the other is a perfect I-system.

The September 11 terrorists professed great belief in God. The central question is whether they were following their I-system or were bridging to God. Bridging to God creates goodness in human behavior. Goodness in behavior and our Source are inseparable. Evil is behavior resulting from a belief in the I-system and following its convoluted requirements. The terrorists' I-systems were filled with requirements such as, "Kill Americans," "God wants Americans dead," "God will reward you richly in heaven if you die fulfilling your mission." These requirements were not bridged toward the Almighty, they were carried out in a meticulously controlled fashion by the I-system.

If the terrorists were bridging to their Source and carrying out God's Will, only compassionate behavior could result. God does not call on us to fulfill our I-system requirements; on the contrary, He calls on us to bridge our I-system and appear before Him naked, stripped of our I-system. God calls out only for good.

COMPASSION

Compassionate behavior comes only from our interface with God. Compassionate behavior is the natural result of decreasing the I-system and expanding our awareness in everyday life. For example, when a baby falls into the shallow end of a swimming pool, we see, we jump, and we rescue. No more, no less—no I-system. But the more a behavior is filtered through our I-system, the less compassionate it is. Morality and pure intentions are rooted in our Source and not dependant on the I-system's view of the outcome. When we are truly intimate with God, cause and effect are inseparable.

Consider what happens to behavior when we bridge the I-system. Our awareness expands, giving us more information, which leads to more appropriate behavior. As the I-system lessens, our subject of awareness lessens. The resulting decrease in self-interest enhances our empathy and the quality of our behavior. The increased flow from body–mind–universe enhances the compassionate nature of our behavior. With continued bridging, the I-system decreases and our circle of awareness expands to greater consciousness. Information becomes *wisdom* and behavior becomes those actions that are required in the moment. Empathy, which is dualistic (I-the-subject empathizes with you-the-object), disappears. Dualistic caring and loving (I love you) also disappear. What is left? Mother Teresa tending the sick and poor. Whether her patients were likeable, lovable, or contagious, her tending was the same. Mother Teresa had no choice in doing what was required in the moment. She loved what her Beloved loves in a non-dualistic way. Her actions were God's Will. Without self-interest and with unlimited consciousness her *actions* were *compassion*.

So the real question is this: How does this consideration of compassion help us out in our everyday lives? First, we know and acknowledge there is a fountain of compassion in all of us that naturally flows outward to seek expression in our deeds. The one and only obstacle to that flow is the I-system. Awareness of the I-system's thoughts is beneficial to our actions. After all, our thoughts are frequently an experimental form of action. The light of awareness lessens the I-system's power and enhances the flow of compassion. Also, gentle, patient, consistent labeling of thoughts and actions gives us more space for more awareness. For example, if you helped yourselves first rather than your guests, you would label that action: "I helped myself first rather than my guests." If you go on to think,

"I wasn't a nice guy," you should continue labeling: "I was thinking, 'I wasn't a nice guy.'" This latter thought may be a central issue in your I-system. Awareness of the I-system's structure increases the likelihood of your actions being compassionate. Finally, in bridging we should consider not only the mental activity but also the body sensations. For example, a deep discomfort in the lower abdomen associated with serving yourself first may indicate a deep I-system requirement about fulfilling your own needs at all costs. Continued awareness is the royal road to compassion.

One question I'm often asked is this: "Should I continue with kind deeds even though I don't want to, or if I have mixed feelings about the kind act? Some related questions are, "What if I have an ulterior motive and am expecting something in return? Am I doing the kind deed just because people will like or respect me?" Remember, we are all rooted in God, and whatever kind deeds we are doing is because of this interface. Second, whatever resistance or contamination we have to kind deeds comes from our I-system. These resistances are all related to the belief in separation. Wanting people to like us, respect us, or do for us is all related to an inner neediness that results from the I-system's basic fiction of separation from our unlimited Source. Finally, with choice-less awareness of our mental and physical activities we supply our own answers. Actions performed when our bodies are relaxed and our minds are calm and in the moment are likely to be in balance and harmony with our *Source*. Bridging is endless and eternal. God is endless and eternal.

THE COLLECTIVE I-SYSTEM

PERSONAL I-SYSTEMS ALWAYS evolve into the collective I-system in group settings. The collective I-system then interferes with the groups functioning and mission. All members of a group are unified by a common mission. The functioning of a group attempts to fulfill its mission. A corporation has a mission to profitably provide services or products. A political party has a mission to get its people elected to public office and to have its platform carried into public policy. A nation has the mission to provide for the safety and welfare of its citizens. A street gang has the mission of dominating a certain area of the city. A church has the mission to bring its congregation closer to God. Every group has a mission and performs functions to accomplish it.

In analogy to the biological system, which represents the natural functioning of the body–mind, we have a natural group system, which represents the natural functions of a group. For example, the natural functions of a doctor's office are scheduling appointments, keeping medical records, billing, taking vital signs, performing physical exams, writing prescriptions, drawing blood, doing lab work, organizing the staff, and so on. These functions enable the practice to fulfill its mission to profitably provide affordable, quality health care.

Let's look at the group dynamic of boy scouts going on a two-week campout to a wilderness area. The leader and his assistants plan the trip, buy the necessary supplies and equipment, and arrange transportation. Each boy packs certain supplies. Some set up tents, other set up the kitchen and latrines, and so on. These are the natural functions of the group. The mission of the natural system is to ensure the health, safety, welfare, and enjoyment of the boy scouts. As long as nearly 100% of the effort is directed toward the mission, there is little collective I-system. Everyone performs his function, and everything flows smoothly.

A troop without a collective I-system would wake up promptly at reveille, dress, wash, make breakfast, eat breakfast, clean up, hike, swim, and so on. Rain or shine, the troop would perform its natural functions and, by so doing, each individual I-system would be lessened. Each boy scout, by sacrificing his individual I-system and choosing to perform natural group functions, would enhance his closeness to the other scouts, the community, nature, and God.

Groups develop a collective I-system because they are

composed of individuals who have I-systems. Each activity of an individual in the group is driven by his or her I-system. Even when performing natural functions of the group, each individual will perform his function in a different way. Frowning, smiling, complaining, and groaning are all I-system behaviors. The development of the collective I-system begins to erode the natural functioning of the group as the collective system begins to usurp natural functions to fulfill its own mission. The core mission of the collective system is always a gathering together of projected individual core beliefs. For example, an individual core belief, "The world will fulfill all my needs," could have a requirement, "Cutting corners will benefit me." This requirement is projected onto the group by individual behaviors, which causes an unconscious resonance with other individual I-systems. If an individual behavior (for instance, cruelty to animals) does *not* resonate with the other I-systems, it will not be incorporated into the collective I-system. If sneaky rule-breaking behavior is in most of the individual I-systems, it will be incorporated into the collective system. Because each individual's behavior is motivated by his I-system, it will carry not only the requirement but also the underlying core belief. Thus, the collective I-system has an identical basic fiction of separation, a unique core belief, and set of requirements, plus a unique strategy for fulfillment. When the collective I-system functions to fulfill its mission, the behaviors it favors will interfere with the natural functioning of the group.

Consider three different boy scout troops. In Troop I, the collective I-system contains the core belief, "The world will fulfill our desires" and the requirement "Cutting corners will make it easy." The group behavior then supports uncooperative, rule-breaking behavior, such as cutting corners in sanitation procedures when troop leaders are not looking. Troop II consists of boy scouts with rebellious behaviors. Their collective I-system would contain requirements full of rebellious requirements challenging authority. They would overtly break rules and bring about open conflict with the scout leaders. Troop III has the requirement "to please authority," which encourages group obedience in hopes that the leader will make it easy on them.

In Troop I, the natural functions of the group will be adversely affected by the collective I-system, as the natural function of looking out for the group's well-being will be adversely affected by shortcuts in sanitation, food prep, and so on. For example, unsanitary conditions could lead to food poisoning. In Troop II, the outward defiant activities will overtly interfere with all the natural functions of the group. In Troop III, the performing of functions to please the leaders inevitably leads to a breakdown in functioning. The scouts eventually will be disappointed because their I-systems' requirements will not be fulfilled. Soon they will lose interest, which then adversely affects the natural functioning of the troop.

So, in all cases the collective I-system interferes with the natural functions of the group. Once the collective I-system is formed, energies of the troop are diverted from doing activities that facilitate the natural mission of the troop and spent on requirements such as fooling the leaders, pleasing the leaders, or challenging the leaders. The

118

leaders then respond with countermeasures. These countermeasures to enforce discipline, detect shortcuts, and maintain control use up more energy. They also become part of the collective I-system. The collective system then grows as the leaders become immersed in a power struggle. Thus, the mission to foster the values, health, safety, and enjoyment of the troop is undermined by the collective I-system.

Bridging the collective I-system is based on the awareness of its structure and functioning. Group tension, gossip, and disturbances of the group's natural functions are signs of a collective I-system. As with individual I-systems, collective systems always restrict awareness, because I-system functioning always draws attention to itself. In bridging the collective system, all members of the group are involved. The collective I-system is fed by individual I-systems, and vice versa. Awareness of the collective system's functioning gives the individuals and the group a choice to follow the system's dictates or to allow the flow of their natural functions. Individual and group awareness of both the material and spiritual face of *reality* is bridging. With continued bridging, all activities of the group become more balanced and in harmony with the Source and all existence.

Let's define a civilization's I-system as the pulling together of a past collective I-system and its dynamic interaction with current individual I-systems. The past collective I-system includes its history, oral tradition, myths, literature, science, arts, codes of behavior, government, and religion. Even though a civilization's I-system may bring cohesiveness and order, it always interferes with the natural functioning of the group and separates individuals in the group from their Source and all existence. Bridging the civilization's I-system frees the natural functioning of the group and allows true compassionate to flow.

Part III
Completion

THE RUBBER HITS THE ROAD

NOW COMES THE TIME to put our findings to work. Every idea, every concept, every understanding, no matter how deep, can become embedded in the I-system. What we have learned so far will be limited unless we diligently apply it in practice. Generally, practice is the repeated activities of the body–mind to gain or express proficiency. For example we perform physical exercise to acquire strength, endurance, and agility, and a doctor practices medicine as an expression of proficiency. If we believe the I-system's conception of ourselves as limited, separate, and needy, we practice to achieve personal goals. But from the point of view of the true self, which is unlimited and overflowing, practice is always an expression of our body–mind functioning, in harmony and balance with *reality*.

Practice is bridging. Practice always rests on a physical base, with the body unified with mind. In that way, body–mind–universe expresses its union with its Source.

What we've discussed until now is like looking at a new car. It smells good, looks good, and feels good—but the real test is when the rubber hits the road. Unfortunately, the analogy stops here. Test driving a new car is thrilling, exciting, and fulfills our I-system's requirements. Bridging is simple and plain; in fact, newcomers often describe it as boring. The true self does not have requirements to fulfill, it simply *is*. Expectations the I-system has about our true selves are false. All of them are just concepts, just thoughts. Remember, the goals of the I-system are to fulfill its requirements. It often uses "feeling good" as a guide. Aside from being present and expressing our true selves in the moment, bridging has no goal. It may be pleasant or unpleasant. We are always present and functioning, otherwise we would not exist—thus, there is nothing to accomplish and nowhere to go.

Again, bridging is no more and no less than being present and functioning in the moment. Our practice is no more and no less than being present and functioning in this moment. Our true self, God, Jesus, Buddha, Allah and *universal consciousness* are all present and functioning in the moment. Complete joy, peace of mind, intelligence, and compassion are also present; the I-system is not. None of our dualistic expectations, hopes, plans, wishes, frustrations, happiness, and suffering is present; only what is *real* and *true* is in the moment. The statement in the *A Course in Miracles* sums up bridging: "Nothing real can be threatened, nothing unreal exists. Herein lies the peace of God." [27]

Although most of us would enthusiastically vote for bridging, many of us will not follow through with the practices I will suggest in this section. The I-system, the cause of our fears and suffering, will cause many of us to refuse to take the walk. The system loves the talk but it can't stand the walk. Too hard, too painful, too simple, too slow, not fun, not exciting, no tangible rewards, plus a thousand other well-reasoned excuses not to practice.

You can read this book in a number of hours, bridging is a never-ending activity. Being in the moment is eternal. Bridging is simply bringing ourselves back to being present again and again. When the I-system causes us to wander, we gently bring ourselves back to the present with choice-less awareness. If it feels good or bad, if it is easy or hard, if we like it or not, we just bring ourselves to where we are *real*, to the present moment.

The only resistance to practice is the I-system. All of the techniques and methods here are meant to deal with the I-system. But returning again and again to being present in the moment is the most effective of all techniques, because *the I-system cannot function in the moment*. Of course, in reality we are always in the moment; but the I-system contracts our awareness and limits our experiencing of this truth.

Practice is like standing on the center of a seesaw and balancing from one side to the other. Sometimes we drift

---

27. *A Course in Miracles*, (Roscoe, NY: Foundation for Inner Peace, 1975), p. 1.

off into our I-system's drama, and the seesaw rests on the ground on one side. It's safe and easy, but it is not our life, which is dynamically active all the time. On the other hand, drifting off or daydreaming is like static stability on the other side—safe and easy, but asleep. Practice is a dynamic stability constantly shifting from the left to right—balance and unbalance. Being in the center of the seesaw is akin to being dynamically in the moment. Only in the moment can we experience the *truth*, which has no resting point. The *truth* dynamically appears and disappears in each moment.

Early on, it seems our practice is all effort. The I-system has us completely convinced that we do not belong in the moment. We believe our existence is the I-system's drama. In fact, we sometimes experience being in the moment as being cold and alone—whereas the I-system is always ready to make us warm and cuddly with its false hopes and expectations.

It's no wonder the system has such a hold over us. It has us convinced that our practice is cold, hard, and suffering, while it is warm, alive, and happy. It takes many of us a long time to summon the courage to question the I-system's storyline. Many will believe the I-system and refuse to practice. Who wants to be out in the cold? But there are courageous souls willing to challenge the King of the Cognitive Mountain. When we do, the I-system has a stacked deck of cards; if we play with this limited deck, the system always wins. Each time we drift out of the moment, we fall back into the I-system's game. Remember, the only real way to challenge the system is to return again and again to the moment. This is nothing but life.

At the onset of bridging, the I-system seemingly has the upper hand, although a fiction can never prevail over the truth. But of course our culture is one big, collective I-system. Mass media, entertainment, marketing, modern convenience, economy, and even government encourages the system. Bridging does not have tremendous support. Not only our individual I-systems but also society's collective I-systems support the resistance to being present in the moment. In fact, much of society would say being present each moment is boring or dangerous, if not downright cult-like.

Practice is simple, plain, and effective, and yet it's difficult at times. Our true self has only one way: We must return again and again to the moment and express ourselves—whether that's easy or hard. During this time, the I-system will constantly and unmercifully resist. However, the truth always prevails. So, for those courageous enough to continue, let me discuss a number of highlights that occur during bridging.

In the early phase of practice we develop techniques that are useful both in formal practice and in everyday life; we also begin to experience our ground of existence. The former is accomplished by *efforting*; the latter occurs naturally as the I-system's hold on us loosens. However, the more we try to push ourselves to experience our true nature, the more we strengthen the I-system's hold.

When I first started to practice, I asked my teacher how long it would me to become enlightened. My false conception was that enlightenment would be a sudden great burst that would turn my world upside down, and afterward I would be as free as a bird forever, without having to do anything else. He answered, "Several years." I asked, "What if I work diligently?" He responded, "Ten years." I pushed on: "What if I really practiced full time?" He smiled: "Twenty years." Of course, he was referring to my I-system becoming more and more swollen with my expectations and effort.

In practicing, there are experiences that are clearly paradoxical and which the rational mind cannot fathom. These experiences do not come from the I-system's efforting, but from the I-system letting go. These experiences give us small tastes of our true nature. One of these experiences occurred to me not long after I started my practice. At that time I was looking for that "big bang of enlightenment" and I didn't pay much attention to the actual experience. Looking back, however, this experience was partly responsible for my continuing practice, despite long periods of no apparent progress. Nothing in my life felt like it was going right, and nothing could console me. Without anything else to do, I began just sitting quietly. I felt lonely. Even though I felt that being alone was one of my great strengths, the loneliness I experienced during my sitting practice was painful. As my thinking subsided, I became aware of how lonely I really *felt*. Suddenly, I became anxious and fearful. Not knowing what to do, I just stayed with my loneliness and fearfulness. It was difficult, but there was no better alternative. After an hour or so, much to my amazement, I felt better. Although nothing remarkable had happened to me, the emptiness and aloneness seemed to be providing a support. I realized that the less thinking I did during my sitting practice, the more support I felt in my everyday life. This became a pleasant time for me, because I felt I did not have to do anything and the support was still there. Soon thereafter, this phase passed.

Being supported by nothing I did—can you see the paradox? The closer to "no thinking" I got during practice, the more support I felt. My support did not come from my limited I-system but from my unlimited, true self. My support—"no thinking and no doing"—was exactly opposite to my I-system, which could only support by thinking and doing. The I-system cannot "will" itself to not think; therefore, the support must come from a force outside of the system—from the *life force, true self, ground of existence,* God. This *life force* is our natural endowment. Only the I-system can fool us into thinking, "God is not there."

Disembodiment is being so caught up in our mental functions that we are insensitive and unaware of our bodies.[28] The body is constantly alive with changing sensations everywhere, yet we typically are unaware of its ever-present fullness and vitality. But when we've been practicing awhile and our body–mind is aligned, relaxed, and resilient, we begin to experience light, transient sensations that usually start in our faces or hands and later flow into and out of our bodies. The body becomes relaxed. Thoughts become clearer and slower but, more importantly, begin drifting freely in and out of awareness. The

---

28. Will Johnson, Change, Transformation, and the Universal Pattern of Myofascial Holding (Unpublished paper).

usual tension that accompanies our thinking dissipates. Sensations, perceptions, and thoughts seem to be harmoniously unified. The duality of mind/body lessens as our mind pervades our body. Being present in the moment seems natural, almost effortless. We are experiencing *body–mind consciousness*. This natural expansion of consciousness allows us to experience our true selves and become more intimate with God. This phase comes and goes; it may last seconds, minutes, or hours.

The settledness of our formal practice then carries over into our everyday lives, where we have a sense of calmness and tranquility in the midst of our everyday turmoil. Gradually, we become more grounded in our bodies. With continuing awareness of our mental and physical activities, our personal drama lessens and we become more responsive to life's situations rather than our self-centered activities. Life itself is the only teacher.

In more advanced stages of practice, we experience a state I call *presence*. In addition to the ever-changing *presencing* of the physical world, we begin to experience an unchanging, underlying calmness and tranquility in our body–mind. As our practice continues, this *presence* becomes clearer, with the ever-changing world in the foreground and the unchanging harmony and balance in the background; but the *presence* is still dualistic, because foreground and background are two. At some point finally, the ever-changing *presencing* of the world and the underlying calmness and tranquility merge and *we are present and functioning*. Everyday life and the ground of existence are *one*. Washing dishes, cleaning the toilet, working at our job, and making love are all embraced equally. We are always *present and functioning* in the midst of our ever-changing everyday life.

BRIDGING PRACTICES

Let me offer some suggestions for those who want to pursue bridging practice. By describing these techniques, I'm not excluding other practices that are also successful for bridging the I-system. Because life is complex, we need as much help as possible to see into our true nature—so here are some of my suggestions.

First, sit still. In surgery, the doctor tries to limit one of the variables, bacterial contamination, by ensuring a sterile field. By assuming the sitting posture, one of the variables we limit is voluntary movement. Another reason to sit still is so we can better observe the need to move and fidget—our restless nature. We may never know how really restless we are until we sit still and quietly observe ourselves. It's like putting a snake in a hollow tube; for the first time, the snake becomes aware of its wiggly nature as its skin rubs against the tube. The sitting posture offers us primetime viewing of our I-system, which is constantly acting, reacting, and interacting with everything in our lives. Indeed, it's a perpetual motion machine and, like the adept magician, it always keeps us distracted. So we need a time and quiet place that's conducive for the I-system to settle. More importantly, the sitting posture with the body–mind harmonized and balanced is a total actualization of *reality*. At that moment, the entire universe is sitting. Of course the entire physical universe is not literally sitting, but we are sitting so complete, so total, so limitless that our body-mind is unified with our Source and all existence. There is no room for separation into sitting and not-sitting. The spiritual universe is sitting. *Reality* is sitting. When our body–mind–universe is harmonized, unified, and balanced, each and every activity of life is *reality*.

Because sitting on a cushion on a floor mat is the most traditional way of practice and is well documented, let me refer interested readers to Will Johnson's book, *The Posture of Meditation*.[29] However, my twenty-five years of sitting practice both on the floor and on a chair have lead me to conclude that chair sitting can be as effective as the traditional method, if you do it properly. Because most traditional literature doesn't focus on chair sitting, I will cover the subject in detail. From my experience and observations, very few chair sitters are guided by the triad of alignment,

---

29. Will Johnson, *The Posture of Meditation* (Boston: Shambhala Publications, 1996).

relaxation and resilience. In fact, until I met Will Johnson, I wasn't guided myself.

Before starting your practice, you should buy two or three 15-by-15-inch, high-density, firm foam squares that are 4 inches thick. These are often samples at foam stores and so are inexpensive. If you do not have the foam squares, you can use cushions or pillows. Next, find a chair that does not have arms or a soft seat. Folding metal or plastic chairs are fine.

I am just over six feet tall, and my anatomy dictates that I use all three foam squares. At first I tried one square, then two, which was almost right, but three was ideal. You may need only one or two. The goal is to have your hips elevated 4 to 8 inches above your knees. That way your weight is distributed in a triangular fashion, where most of your weight is on the sitting bones, with only a little transferred to the feet.

When you first sit this way, it will feel awkward; it's almost like floating—not quite sitting, not quite standing. Although you may feel unstable or like you're about to fall, do not lean against the back of the chair. The unstableness is a great aid in getting to know the body–mind. Try tipping the pelvis back (by moving the upper body backward), so you feel like you're falling over backward. Next tilt your pelvis and upper body forward. Do this very slowly so you can feel the weight being transferred from your sitting bones to your feet. Gently sway your upper body forward and back until you gradually come to a comfortable position with your back relatively aligned with gravity and relaxed. Now sway your upper body to the left and feel the weight shift to the left sitting bone. Do the same to the right. Now sway back and forth with gradually decreasing arcs until you come to a resting position where you feel the pressure equally on each sitting bone. Check to see if there is any undue tension in your back, legs, or neck. If there is tension, just be aware of it; the tension does not need to disappear.

I cannot stress how important this first phase of sitting is. It is crucial that you do your best to feel and experience the pressure on each sitting bone and on each foot. This will help greatly in aligning with gravity. Some may find these pressure sensations difficult to feel. Please be patient and kind to yourself and keep on trying. If you can do the first step, your confidence will grow. Most of us are disembodied in our everyday lives, and this chair sitting exercise is an important beginning. You should do this exercise before each new sitting period; and before you get up from sitting you should sway again to help you carry mindfulness of your body into your everyday life.

Here are some other essential components of sitting:

- Allow your head to be aligned comfortably on your spine so there is no downward or upward tilt of your chin. You should be able to look comfortably forward to a point at about the same level as your eyes.

- Keep your head relaxed and your eyes looking downward at forty-five degrees. Do not tip you head, only lower your gaze.

- As you work with your head, check any tensions

that develop in your neck and back and recheck the pressure on your sitting bones and feet.

- Closing your eyes facilitates sleepiness and you need to be wide awake to practice. In general, it is better to keep your eyes opened, relaxed and not glancing about. When your eyes are darting about, your I-system is active.

- Place your hands palm down on each thigh; this will help you feel the balance as you sway from left to right and back and forth. Experiment and see for yourself how the pressure on your hands helps you sense the balancing of you body. If you feel quite a bit of pressure on your fingers, you are leaning too far forward. Remember, however, that your hands are not meant to act as supports, only as sensors.

- At some time in the future you may want to experiment with another hand position. First, place your right hand with the palm up on your lap; then place the left hand palm up on top, so that the corresponding fingers are almost in line with each other. Your thumbs should be moved closer so that they just touch each other. Both thumbs and the adjoining fingers then make an oval.

  This hand position lets you gauge your mind's activity by focusing on your thumbs. Initially they will just touch so that a piece of paper could be held in place between them. When your mind is tense, however, your thumbs will push harder together. On the other hand, when your mind is sleepy or wandering, your thumbs will drift apart. I suggest you start with your hands palm down on the thighs for a while, because it aids body balance and awareness.

That covers our triad of tools: alignment with mindfulness of gravity, relaxation with mindfulness of muscle tension and body sensations, and resilience with mindfulness of allowing the body's natural movement with our breathing. Using the back support of the chair does not allow your body to sway and restricts resilience. All bodies maintain postural alignment with gravity with small, involuntary sways that usually are beyond our awareness. When the triad is in place, we can fully experience our aliveness and vitality.

When your are first chair sitting it is best to start by being mindful of the sensations of your body. Being mindful of sounds is also very important. If your breathing is shallow, labored, or rapid, just observe—don't try to fix it. Your breathing will take care of itself if your I-system doesn't meddle too much. A period of shallow, labored, rapid breathing is as good as a period of deep, relaxed, slow breathing. The I-system may believe that time spent sunbathing in Hawaii is more valuable than time spent cleaning the house, but in *reality* one period of time is as good as the other. Until you experience this firsthand you may disagree, but "life as it is" is our only teacher.

Bridging starts with an aspiration for truth, to see for yourself what this life is about. For practice to begin, the aspirations, our life force, must overcome the I-system's resistance. Deep inside, we seek the truth, even if it means opposing the I-system. Out of the conflict to see the truth on one hand and continue our fiction on the other, we grow. We want to practice—we don't want to practice, both at the same time. Do we say, "Why this? Why do I have to practice?" and quit. Or do we gently label our thoughts and go back to our awareness for even a second before being pulled away again. Pulled away again, returning again and again. After all your heart doesn't quit pumping because it doesn't feel like it.

Fueled by our aspirations, continuing practice leads to expanding awareness. There is no correlation between effort and this expanding awareness. It is the practice, not our effort, that gives results. In fact, as I mentioned earlier, effort only strengthens the I-system, which restricts our expanding awareness. As our awareness expands, our belief in the thoughts of the I-system lessens. The I-system keeps putting out thoughts; our practice is not to stop thinking but to return to the present moment, where our attachment to these thoughts, ideas, and discriminations lessens. Bridging is no more and no less than that.

THREE TOOLS

WE CAN DEVELOP A simple way of handling mental phenomena by extending the three tools I mentioned before: alignment, relaxation, and resilience.

- *Alignment.* Physically, we sense gravity and align ourselves exactly opposed to its force. Mentally, we sense the I-system's force of attraction or repulsion on thoughts, body sensations, and perceptions; and we align ourselves exactly opposed to the pressure by allowing these thoughts, sensations, and perceptions to come and go freely. When we experience ourselves physically tipping, we gently allow ourselves to align exactly opposite to gravity; in that position, we can relax, right ourselves, and come to be supported by our spine. When we experience mental tipping—that is, being dragged back into the I-system's drama of thoughts and emotions—we relax, right ourselves with mindfulness, and become supported in the moment by our ground of existence, our life force. Just as there is a life force that allows a tree to grow and be supported exactly opposed to gravity, our own life force allows us to grow and be supported exactly opposed to the I-system. Could a mother bird talk her chicks out of believing they can fly away and resist gravity? Yet the I-system talks us out of our right to fly away from its pull and into God's arms. Not only can we fly away, we can go into orbit around the I-system. In fact, if we get far enough from its grasp, we see the I-system for what it is: a bunch of thoughts that we believe—nothing more or less. At times, we can even smile warmly at its antics.

- *Relaxation:* Physically, relaxation occurs when our muscular system is relatively free of tension. Mentally, relaxation occurs when our mental apparatus is relatively free of tension—that is, when it's freed from the I-system's self-centered thoughts. Again, alignment and relaxation work with awareness rather than force. We can't make the mind be still. Playing with thoughts gives them more energy. Trying to push thoughts out of our mind or to cut them off gives them energy. The only way is to allow our life's awareness to melt them away. Bridging is shining a light of awareness onto the I-system. As our awareness expands and the increased spaciousness occurs, the I-system's hold on us loosens.

Another technique that expands awareness is labeling our thoughts. I'm thinking, "I'll never follow through with this." I'm thinking, "It's time for chocolate." Labeling our thoughts not only lessens the I-system's drama but allows us the space to choose whether to believe a particular thought. Usually we are so sucked in by the I-system we believe that our entire being is limited and defined by our thoughts. Remember that choice-less awareness of all our sensory fields enhances our perception of the world. Awareness of our body sensations allows us to experience the aliveness and vitality of our bodies.

- **Resilience.** Physically, resilience means being flexible enough to allow realignment when physical forces (such as breathing movements, gravity) and forces outside the body–mind act upon us. Mentally, resilience means being flexible and elastic when the I-system impresses its drama upon us. Perhaps a car outside honks its horn while we are doing our sitting practice. Then we start thinking, "What is he doing? Why doesn't he ring the doorbell? I was doing great until that horn, now I'm upset. I'm pissed!" Resilience means we hear "honk, honk" and go back to being aware of our breath moving through our nostrils into our lungs, go back to whatever bodily sensations accompany the honking episode. Resilience means being flexible, coming back to a neutral position of mindfulness in the moment.

  Resilience has a further and critical meaning in

mental functioning. In downhill skiing, if your become comfortable with your position in a turn, you
may hold onto that position for support. Then, you
are woefully unprepared for the changes needed for
the next turn. In the mental field, clinging and
holding onto experiences impairs your resilience,
too. Clinging to past thoughts, memories, and experiences to support us in this very moment will always fail. The I-system cannot support us in the
present moment with its conceptions of past and future. The only true support is our presence and
functioning in the moment. Truth and reality are living in the moment and have no form or substance
which the I-system can grasp.

"WHO?"

BEFORE I INTRODUCE THE "Who?" technique, let's review some of the bridging techniques we've seen.

- Returning to being present in the moment allows us to interrupt and weaken the function of the I-system.

- Labeling thoughts and actions allows us to be less identified with and have less belief in the I-system.

- Experiencing fears and anxieties without trying to alter the thoughts or body sensations interupts I-system functioning and loosens its hold over us.

These techniques allow us to see the structure (made up of personality, requirements, and core beliefs) as well as the functioning (how fears activate the personality, requirements, and core beliefs) of the I-system. This gives us new choices and more opportunities for being present in the moment. As our I-system lessens, our awareness expands and the belief in the separate *I* decreases.

The "Who?" technique is helpful in quiet bridging practice. For example, when you are being constantly drawn away from being present in the moment, you can silently ask, "Who?"—meaning, "Who is pulling me away from the moment?" You are asking for the separate, self-subsistent, unchanging *I*, who lives in the past or future, to *presently step forward*. The "Who?" should be subtle enough so all of your senses are wide open. Allowing the inquiry, you quietly watch. When you are pulled away again, you ask "Who?" Then return to your usual practice of choice-less awareness. This allows you to question your belief in a separate *I*. You continue to question until there is no longer a question. This technique works over time.

The "Who?" techinique is also helpful in bridging practices of everyday life. When you are dissapointed with your life, you ask, "Who is it that is dissatisfied?" and return to your body sensations and everyday life. When the momentary burst of colors on your retina at sunset is reduced to thoughts such as, "This sunset was almost as good as the one in Hawaii," we gently ask, "Who took away this sunset?"

As you continue to ask "Who?" you are bridging the I-system, and *reality* answers you with just "This!" "This!" is *reality* here and now experienced with a resting I-system. As bridging continues, you come to experience "Who?" with the entire body–mind–universe. "Who?"

dissolves into the ineffable *Source*, and our everyday life continues.

KNOTS:

DOING AND UNDOING

T HE I-SYSTEM FUNCTIONS by incessantly spinning thoughts and increasing body tension. Like a knot, it causes discomfort and disharmony, and is difficult to undo. In fact, if we try to undo the knots through effort, the knot only gets tighter. Because knots are unpleasant, the I-system attempts to fix the situation by contracting our awareness and focusing on pleasant thoughts. This makes it difficult to be present in the moment. In fact, without knots, it would be quite natural for us to be present in the moment Bridging is simply returning again and again to mindfulness of our mental and physical experiences. At first, we may be aware only of the spinning thoughts and not of our body sensations because of our contracted awareness. Chronic tension anesthetizes our bodies. We are unaware

146

of all the tensions our bodies carry throughout life. We believe this is the normal state. It is only when awareness is repeatedly returned to our body that we become aware of our chronic tension and holding patterns, our knots. As our awareness becomes less restricted, we begin experiencing the body's discomfort, which we previously denied. When this first happens, we feel like we are taking a step backward. We falsely believe that our awareness is causing the discomfort. As we bring our awareness again and again to the present moment, however, our body's knots become more evident and our spinning thoughts slow. Understanding the knots brings only limited results. Returning awareness again and again to the present moment is the only way to loosen them. When the mental knots loosen, the mind becomes more peaceful and the body knots tend to be replaced with a lightness. Practice is simply being aware of our physical and mental activities in each moment.

After you have been bridging for a while, you'll have periods when your thoughts are slowed and your body relaxed. At other times, it will be difficult to return yourself to the present moment. The present moment is like a wild bronco, bucking and tossing us here and there. Each return could be full of effort. You might be tempted to conclude that the present moment is an unfriendly, unpleasant place. The truth of the matter is that the present moment is your only true resting place. The present moment is the only place in the world where we can function freely and have peace of mind.

Labeling thoughts during chair sitting practice and everyday life is one effective tool for bridging. If a thought arises in our mind and we do not expand our awareness and label it, that thought can become a requirement of the I-system, filling our body-mind with anxiety and tension. But, by expanding our awareness and labeling that thought, we can prevent the I-system from confiscating that though; we can use if freely with a relaxed body-mind. Labeling not only helps us to see emotions as just plain thoughts and bodily sensations, but enables us to start mapping out the I-system. Mapping is simply awareness of what our requirements and core beliefs are (structure) and how they work (function). For instance, seeing the thought, "I want to be in control" as an I-system requirement that causes anxiety and tension is important. As time goes on, you become aware of the system's complex strategy for maintaining this requirement and you come to see its relationship to your personality. Later, you realize how these requirements are related to just about everything you do in life. It becomes clear that most of your tension is related to the nature of your requirements rather than the to nature of life. As the tension and anxiety decrease, the I-system melts and your awareness continues to expand. Seeing the connection between the controlling requirement and the core belief (such as, "The world will fulfill my needs") takes time. As you recall, core beliefs are fueled by your basic fiction of separation and mobilize all your requirements. Finally, remember that bridging does not have a specific goal, such as mapping the structure and functioning of the I-system. Instead, bridging is choice-less awareness of whatever is present in each moment.

What I have been describing thus far is mainly *efforting*

on our part. We are trying to expand our awareness by returning again and again to the present moment. We are also labeling thoughts and becoming aware of the function and structure of the I-system. You might be tempted to conclude that conscious efforting will be counterproductive to bridging because it strengthens the I-system. And if you were efforting to achieve something you don't already have in the moment, that would be true. However, this very moment, you are fully connected to your Source with ample peace of mind and fulfillment. Efforting to become Michael Jordan, Bill Gates, or Oprah Winfrey only reinforces your I-system. Efforting to expand your awareness to experience what you already have—your true self—is bridging.

As you continue to practice, you begin to experience efforts and activities that are beyond the grasp of your cognitive mind. The I-system cannot function when your mind is quiet and your body relaxed. In those periods, your awareness naturally expands and you experience your body–mind non-dualistically—that is, not as a separate object. Earlier, I described this state as *body–mind consciousness,* in which we experience ourselves as embodied. The envelope of awareness expands outward without any conscious effort on our part. Our true self is unveiling itself to us. God is blessing us. With this expanded awareness, we experience the I-system's requirements and core beliefs as just thoughts; they have less grip on our awareness and less ability to create knots. When a thought like "I need to be in control" surfaces, our body remains relaxed, and the anxiety signal is not activated. The I-system is dissolving!

When this occurs, you may experience your body as lighter, because it is not weighed down by the I-system's tension. You experience your mind as clear and ready for everyday life. These pleasant states are due to the lightening of your I-system. Your expanding awareness is less and less dependent on efforts to clarify the I-system or to return to the moment. As time goes on, you become accustomed to these states, which you then experience as nothing special. These states of expanded awareness and clarity will come and go, sometimes with effort, sometime without particular effort on your part. Bridging is doing and not doing, and beyond doing and not doing. Acts of loving kindness will flow naturally. Each moment becomes a full, complete, and total expression of who you are.

EVERYDAY *LIFE*

BRIDGING IS SIMULTANEOUSLY running to our Source and returning to everyday life. We experience the calmness and quietness of being held by our Source along with the clamor and activity of everyday life. Although we have free will, cause and effect holds us responsible for our actions. Our Source is clear and bright, but the I-system prevents us from being in harmony and balance with it. In everyday life, bridging is beyond effort and not efforting. We continue efforting for purity until it is effortless. Each moment is not only an opportunity for a mistake but an opportunity for compassion to bloom. Bridging is beyond mistakes and non-mistakes. The following simple exercise is useful for everyday life.

During everyday life, events that "push your buttons" are the most useful for bridging. When you are faced with circumstances that make you feel angry, spiteful, helpless, weak, anxious, or ashamed, you have an opportunity for bridging. Whenever the circumstances permit, try using the "stop, look, and listen" exercise.

"Stop" your exclusive attachment and total identification with your personal drama, then "look and listen" to all of your senses. Starting with your body, begin sensing your alignment with gravity and become aware of muscle tensions in your head, neck, shoulders, and back. Be mindful of visceral sensations, such as a lump in the throat, a dry mouth, a tight stomach, a racing heart, or rapid breathing. Experiencing all these various sensations will ground you in reality.

Usually we are so focused on the event that pushed our buttons that we neglect the big picture of simultaneously being tuned into all sensations, perceptions, and thoughts. If we do tune in, we can experience our angry thoughts being dissolved in the ocean of expanded body–mind–universe. Our I-system loses a little grip over us when we experience our bodily sensations simultaneously with our disturbing thoughts.

It may only take a few seconds to "stop, look, and listen." Sitting practice provides the foundation for "stop, look, and listen," but without our everyday life experiences to guide us, practice is useless.

CONFESSIONS AND BEHAVIOR

ALL OF US HAVE SINCERELY apologized for a behavior, and then found ourselves doing the same thing again. Saying "I'm sorry" and making confessions don't seem to help much in making a change. Feelings of guilt and remorse don't alter our behavior. How often have we seen repentance without changing our ways? Punishment, even in the criminal justice system, does little to reduce recidivism.

So explore the meaning of *confession*. The Latin roots are *com*, which means together, and *fateria*, which means to acknowledge. Generally, we focus on the second root and neglect the first. When a person does not admit to doing something, we say, "She needs to 'fess up." It seems most of us use confession only as an admission of fact. Seen in this way, it's no wonder confession does little to change our behavior. In reality, it's the first root—con, meaning *together*—that is the key to changing behavior. Our I-system allows us to "fess up," but it resists togetherness. As long as the I-system is robust, all the confessions, apologies, and punishments in the world will not alter our behavior.

Another definition of confession is to declare belief. *Webster's Unabridged Dictionary* uses Matthew 10:32 as an example: "Whosoever therefore shall confess me before man, him I confess also before my Father in heaven." For belief to be total and true, the I-system must be melted down. For us to receive lasting atonement with God, we must have a diminished I-system and be together with God—we must have *at-one-ment*. The I-system's mission of separation resists this altogether.

Consider an everyday example of spending too much money and then telling our mate, "I'm sorry." After the apology, we continue with the same behavior. We "fessed up," but we did not confess. It is possible for the I-system to change its requirements and spend less, of course; but, the I-system itself will not be diminished, and the appropriateness and compassion of our behavior will not change. A real confession would be a major undertaking of mindfully experiencing the nature of our I-system. A strong aspiration to seek the truth of our existence, along with a strong bridging practice that expands into our everyday life, would be a helpful start to this process.

Of course, changing our spending habits is not the goal of bridging. That goal will only enhance our I-system. Instead, we must include the behavior of spending too much into all aspects of our awareness practice. During sitting practice, we include and label our thoughts of spending and having a good time shopping. As we return to choice-less awareness, we may become aware of body sensations such as abdominal aching and neck tension. Sad and painful thoughts may also appear. Bridging is returning again and again to the present moment of our thoughts, perceptions, and sensations.

During daily life, we continue labeling our spending thoughts and being mindful of our activities. We may come to experience intense discomfort as we do not act out our spending thoughts. The pleasant spending thoughts may be replaced by thoughts of being needy and unfulfilled. The more we can resist the spending urges, the more our awareness will expand to previously hidden workings of our I-system. Even though we might slip into periods of overspending, our increasing mindfulness of the body–mind activity before, during, and after the behavior reduces the I-system.

As the I-system is melting, we may become aware of its structure and functioning. We see our complex strategy for spending-justification or for minimizing the adverse effects of overspending. Underlying our requirement may be the core belief, "The world will fulfill all my needs." Layers of disappointment, sadness, and anger may well be uncovered with continuing bridging. But as our consciousness expands to include how the I-system works, its ability to capture awareness, arouse anxiety, and create tension in our body decreases. Spending thoughts now come and go as our requirements, core beliefs, and thoughts of separation become less dominant. We come together with our true self, which doesn't have a neediness to fulfill by spending. Body–mind–universe meets body–mind–universe as awareness becomes *knowing* that flows into our everyday behavior.

TEN COMMANDMENTS

LET'S LOOK AT THE Ten Commandments from the standpoint of bridging. In Exodus 20:1 through 20:11, note that the first four commandments describe our relationship with God. In Exodus 20:12 through 20:14, the remaining commandments deal with the relationship among people. With this framework, let me offer the following commentary on Exodus 20:1 through 20:11:

God is absolute and indivisible. Therefore, when the I-system conceptualizes God, it can only grasp the knowable part. If we believe in that conceptualization, we have a false image. We cannot *know* God through our dualistic I-system. But we can *know* our Creator nondualistically when our I-system rests. With resting I-system and expanding consciousness, bridging occurs and true worship is possible. Sabbath, like the resting I-system, is holy.

Following the first four Commandments means *knowing*. Following the remaining Commandments means *compassion*. Knowing is not *knowing* unless *compassion* flows. *Compassion* cannot flow without *knowing*. Our only obstacle is the I-system. We not only have to rest the I-system but also reduce its power with continuing mindfulness and appropriate actions. The Ten Commandments are a whole, and we must consider all parts simultaneously for *wholeness*.

Each witness present at Sinai was filled with awe as their I-systems rested. To experience and express the *truth* of the Commandments today, the I-system must be at rest and our consciousness expanded, just as it was for those of who witnessesed the original Sinai event. Prayer and associated ritual points us in the direction of the *transcendent* and reduces the I-system's fiction of separation. However, if we worship I-system concepts rather than God, the I-system becomes stronger. The nature of the mind is to form concepts; if the concept is pointing us toward appreciation of *truth*, the I-system will rest and our consciousness will expand. The study of the New Testament, the Torah, and other holy texts can either increase or decrease the I-system. If the aim of our study is to *grasp* the *unknowable,* then our I-system will swell with pride. Conversely, if the study expands our openness, appreciation, and awareness of the *unknowable*, then the I-system rests. Dancing, singing, and rhythmic movements may expand our awareness to *body–mind consciousness*. But if their purpose is to make the I-system feel good, the I-system will expand. Conversely, if the purpose is to use our body–mind to experience God's gifts in our everyday life, the I-system is bridged.

Be mindful that the I-systems can later gobble up those experiences and create food for thought, which will lead to worshipping the experience rather than the Creator. These experiences then satisfy the I-system's requirements and reinforce its storyline, which restricts our awareness. We then worship our fiction. Bridging brings us back to our purpose of true worship.

SPIRITUAL BYPRODUCTS

BRIDGING IS NOT ABOUT spiritual or mystical highs. It's not about out-of-body or otherworldly experiences. It's not about sensing enlightenment or the brain changes that occur during intense or long periods of meditation. *Bridging is about being present and functioning in this very moment.* Bridging never leaves this very moment to go on a trip— not even one to spiritual bliss. Bridging is about everyday life. It is experiencing the *truth* of our existence and expressing that *truth* while we are washing dishes or talking to our neighbor.

Bridging uses the body–mind to simultaneously experience, unify, and express our place in the *transcendence* and *immanent*. Our feet are always planted in the here and now. In bridging the I-system, we may have a multitude of experiences. Spiritual byproducts are any of the apparent gains that bridging may bring. Because bridging is always in the present moment, we can never gain anything we do not already have. Bridging allows the I-system to recede so that we can experience our natural bounty. Spiritual byproducts are the natural flow of practice as we become more intimate with our Source. Our minds become calmer, we see our lives more clearly, our bodies experience more healing and wellness, our relationships improve, even vocational and financial success may follow. Spiritual byproducts also refer to experiences that occur during bridging which are beyond the usual perceptual-conceptual frame. Lights, tunnels, speaking in tongues, out-of-body or otherworldly experiences, feelings of oneness, and ultra-clarity are a few examples. No matter how overwhelming the experience or the apparent gain, however, the critical point is being mindful of *reality* without neglecting either the material or non-material face. God is present in each moment. You cannot find God by escaping from the here and now.

If our I-system becomes attached to any of these spiritual byproducts, it's no different than being attached to material products such as alcohol and drugs. Because who we are is not dependent on appearances or disappearances, we should appreciate the disappearances or non-appearance of spiritual byproducts as much as we appreciate their appearances. The royal road is bridging the I-system with a lifelong practice. Attachment to spiritual highs or byproducts is a detour.

CONCLUSIONS

Wᴴᴇɴ ᴏᴜʀ ᴇᴠᴇʀʏᴅᴀʏ ʟɪꜰᴇ is grounded in the I-system, our appreciation of life is shallow and always changing. Happiness is transient and without peace of mind. We slavishly scramble after elusive goals targeted by the I-system. When we are fortunate enough to attain a goal, the I-system simply changes the target. Happiness becomes unhappiness. There is no way the I-system can bring us true happiness. Yet, we all are busy chasing, wasting our lives, day after day.

When we are bridging the I-system, we face an immensely different situation. Rather than constantly pulling the world into the I-system for satisfaction, we begin to experience the energy of creation as being alive within us. We begin experiencing this "cup runneth over" energy as coming from everywhere and creating everything. The limited *I* fades and is replaced by our true self. The true self simultaneously realizes its place in the *transcendent* and in the *immanent*. This place is right here, right now, in this very moment. We simultaneously experience the support of God and participate in the magnificence of everyday life. In each moment, life is as it is: washing dishes, sweeping the floor, tossing a ball, making love, and working long hours.

What becomes of the I-system? The basic fiction of separation on which the system is founded—"*I* am separate, unchanging, and self-subsistent"—is *seen* by every cell, organ, and system in our body–mind for what it is: nothing more or less than mere thoughts. We may or may not continue to have those thoughts. The basic fiction may be likened to the thought, "I am a jet pilot," which I believed as I played as a young boy. During play, this thought controlled my awareness and directed my body–mind's activities. Today, if I had the same thought, it wouldn't affect my activities. The limited *I,* whom we believed was a subject of all awareness, isn't to be found. We cannot *see* the limited *I*. Within each moment, all existence simply *is*. There is no separate *I*. Even though the physical world is present, all existence is equally close to and distant from God. The transformation of the limited *I* into the true self manifests as the golden rule. We "treat others as we want them to treat us" not because of a rule, but because we cannot do anything else. We do not need a limited *I* to show us the way. Our core beliefs, requirements, and strategy fades. The way is realized each moment by our *compassion*. Our thinking is released to realize our innate *wisdom* and *intelligence*.

The key to the I-system's power is its ability to con-fiscate thoughts which control our awareness and create anxiety. With bridging, all of the thoughts that formerly belonged to the I-system lose their ability to restrict our awareness or create anxiety. Without this key, the system is without power. All our thoughts and actions now move naturally, as the I-system finally becomes reintegrated into our biological system.

EPILOGUE:

MAKING THE WORLD A BETTER PLACE

BRIDGING THE I-SYSTEM improves our daily lives and makes the world a better place. It is written for those who do not choose to have a formal practice, as well as those who do. Below is a summary of findings which support these premises:

1) *Reality* has both a material face (the physical world) and a non-material face (the spiritual world). One cannot exist without the other.

2) Navigating through life without awareness of the non-material face causes us suffering, anxiety, tension, and a host of diseases. It impairs our health and our peace of mind.

3) Without awareness of the spiritual world, we are

fooled into thinking that we are separate from our Source and all existence.

4) The I-system is a part of the mind whose existence is built on the fiction of separation. All the activities of our body–mind are influenced by this system. We feel needy, isolated, and suffering, and are actions are self-centered and lack compassion.

5) The I-system can function only with body tension and fear.

6) The I-system rests when we are present in this very moment. The moment is complete and nothing is missing when we experience both its material and its non-material aspects.

7) Personality is a manifestation of the I-system's work of fulfilling its own set of unique requirements.

8) Because the I-system's backbone is fear, giving up or fighting (both literally and figuratively) are its methods of solving problems. The I-system is dualistic: It considers bodies and the the external world as an object to be manipulated.

9) If we don't experience both faces of *reality*, our activities are out of harmony and balance with our Source. The greater the imbalance and disharmony, the greater our suffering—and the greater the world's suffering.

10) Bridging the I-system expands our awareness, so we can experience, unify, and express *reality*. Moment by moment, we are harmonizing and balancing our body–mind with body–mind–universe. Our lives become *compassion in action*.

11) Bridging has a physical, mental, and spiritual base.

First, we harmonize and balance our bodies with our surroundings. Next, we harmonize our minds with our body–mind–universe. Finally, we harmonize our body–mind–universe with *reality* by expressing *compassion*.

12) Our true self, which expresses its place in the *transcendent* and the *immanent* each moment, emerges with bridging. Our true self is not diminished or enhanced by circumstances.

13) Everyone within all religious traditions can bridge. Praying; using rosary beads; studying the Bible, the Torah, the Koran, the Vedas; practicing deeds of loving kindness; worshipping God, Jesus, Buddha, Allah; experiencing quiet periods; meditating; walking in nature —all of these can be bridging.

14) Society is a gathering together of individual I-systems into a collective I-system.

15) Most relationships are clashes of individual I-systems that are thirsting for fulfillment of their own requirements.

16) A country's collective I-systems fulfilling its requirements starts wars.

17) Awareness of society's collective I-system is crucial for the world, because the key to every I-system is separation and fear. Evil decreases with bridging our individual and collective I-systems.

18) Most religions are united by worshipping one God; they are separated only by personal and collective I-systems.

I hope I have shown you the importance of bridging for our mental, physical, and spiritual well-being. Seeing our I-systems in action in everyday life gives us ever-new behavioral choices. The world needs new ways of seeing itself. Bridging can help.

STANLEY H. BLOCK, MD, is Adjunct Professor of Law and Psychiatry at Seattle University School of Law and Board Certified in Psychiatry and Psychoanalysis. He has had academic appointments and taught at a number of medical schools, including his alma mater UCLA. Before entering medical school, he received an M.A. in physics at the University of California, Berkeley. Dr. Block is currently developing medical applications based on Bridging the I-System philosophy. He lives in University Place, Washington with his wife and collaborator Carolyn Bryant Block. Visit www.bridgingtheisystem.com for more information on his work.